in GOD'S HANDS

PATSY PEARSON

The Story of One Couple,
Inseparable in Ministry and in Life

4square books

In God's Hands © copyright 2020 by Patsy Pearson.

All rights reserved. No part of this book may be reproduced in any form whatsoever, by photography or xerography or by any other means, by broadcast or transmission, by translation into any kind of language, nor by recording electronically or otherwise, without permission in writing from the author, except by a reviewer, who may quote brief passages in critical articles or reviews.

ISBN: 978-1-61766-287-4

Scriptures taken from the Holy Bible, New International Version®, NIV®. Copyright © 1973, 1978, 1984, 2011 by Biblica, Inc.™ Used by permission of Zondervan. All rights reserved worldwide. www.zondervan.com The "NIV" and "New International Version" are trademarks registered in the United States Patent and Trademark Office by Biblica, Inc.®

Lyrics for "Another Soldier's Coming Home" used with permission of Janet Paschal.

Cover design by Rebecca Pagel
Cover photograph by the author
Outline map of Indonesia by xileodesigns

Published 2020 by Chris Fayers under the imprint of
4 Square Books
Stillwater, Minnesota
maenadest@protonmail.com

Printed in the United States of America

Dedication

For Mom and Dad.

You made me what I am. Mom, your curiosity and interest in everything influenced me to become a lifelong learner, and your optimism helped me to see the glass half full and to look for the beauty around me. Dad, your determination and hard work was an inspiration to me, and your faith in me taught me to reach higher and do my best. Thank you for teaching me about God and His love for me so I could accept that love for myself. In the process of writing this book, I have felt as if the two of you were keeping me company. I was sad when I finished writing, but I'm looking forward to seeing you again in heaven. I love you both!

Contents

Introduction		9
Prologue		11
Chapter 1	The Early Years	13
Chapter 2	Starting in Ministry: The Preparation	27
Chapter 3	Heading for Indonesia	37
Chapter 4	Arrival and Settling In	45
Chapter 5	Bandjarmasin	49
Chapter 6	Bandjarmasin Again: Second Term	72
Chapter 7	More Time in Sulawesi: Third Term	112
Chapter 8	Planting Churches in Central Java: Fourth Term	128
Chapter 9	Just the Two of Them Again: Fifth Term	137
Chapter 10	The Moluccan Islands: Sixth Term	149
Chapter 11	Much Work, Illness, and Visitors: Seventh Term	156
Chapter 12	Moluccas and West Papua: Eighth Term	161
Chapter 13	Central Sulawesi: Ninth Term	169
Chapter 14	Sumatra: Tenth Term	177
Chapter 15	Central Sulawesi and Irian Jaya: Eleventh Term	182
Chapter 16	Saying Goodbye	188
Epilogue		195
Acknowledgements		199
Glossary of Indonesian Words		200
Indonesian Place Names		201

Introduction

When you're growing up, it's easy to take your parents for granted, along with the things they did and accomplished. However, when I began going through forty years' worth of my mom's letters, along with her meticulous logbooks, I had a growing realization that this story needed to be told. It's a story of two people who loved one another deeply and together were wholeheartedly devoted to God.

It was His call upon their lives that led them to the beautiful country of Indonesia to take the good news of His salvation to the Indonesian people. They gave up many things: proximity to family and friends, comforts of American life, and certainty about the future. They traded those things for a life often filled with hardships, uncertainty, and even danger—all for the inestimable joy of seeing lives changed and made new in Christ.

They didn't think of themselves as anything out of the ordinary, but simply obedient servants of God. This is the story of what God can do through people who are obedient to Him, who trust Him with their care and protection as they place themselves in His Hands.

Prologue

May 2, 1946

With the salty spring breeze rustling our hair, our clothing, we stood on the deck of the ocean liner: my parents, Harold and Jean Carlblom, my big sister Joanne, baby Marjorie in my mom's arms, and me. I was five, and this was my biggest adventure ever. We waved at the friends who stood far below on the San Francisco dock, bidding us farewell as we embarked on a new life. This was the beginning of Mommy and Daddy's dream—their "life's calling," as they used to say. They were heading out in missionary service to Indonesia—with three children in tow. There had been a slight delay. The *S.S. Monterey* of the Matson Line, which was to sail at 4:00 p.m. the afternoon before, had been delayed and didn't leave until 7:00 the next morning. Long awaited and blasting loud, the ship's horn signaled the impending departure. The ship left its mooring and set sail for a destination halfway around the world. As we slipped under the Golden Gate Bridge, we took our final long look at the last of the United States that we would see for almost four years.

Chapter 1

The Early Years

All the days ordained for me were written in your book before one of them came to be. —Psalm 139:16

Harold's story began in 1913 in the little farming town of Terry, in eastern Montana. Harold Robert was the second of six children born to Albert and Anna Carlblom. The couple had moved to Montana shortly after their marriage because of an offer of free land for homesteads, but they soon found out the area was better suited to ranching than farming.

When Harold was eight or nine, the family moved back to Hopkins, Minnesota, which had better farm conditions than Montana. Harold's days were filled

Earl and Harold taking their heifers to the fair.

with school and farm chores. He raised a Jersey heifer and Poland China pigs for the 4-H club, winning ribbons at the county fair and then going on to the state fair. Harold enjoyed showing his animals at the fairs because he took pride in the results of his hard work, but he also enjoyed the attention from the pretty girls!

Harold expected to follow his dad's footsteps in farming, and after tenth grade he attended the University of Minnesota School of Agriculture during 1929–1930.

Harold had been confirmed in the Lutheran faith as a youth but didn't have a heart encounter with God until he was 17. A neighbor, Herman Hagemeister, offered him the chance to earn some money by helping with plowing on the Hagemeister farm. The Hagemeisters held a regular prayer meeting in their home and one day invited Harold to attend. It was a meeting that would change his life. During prayer, the realization came that he had never given his heart to the Lord. Right then and there he then accepted Christ as his Savior. Harold must have felt a call to the ministry right away because he wanted to go to Bible school immediately; but he was advised by the Hagemeisters to wait until he had turned 18.

Jean's Story

Jean was born in Winnipeg, Canada, on August 11, 1912, to Louis and Robina Ramsay. Louis had emigrated to Canada from Scotland as a young man and found work as a china salesman. He met Robina Low, whom he called "Kiddy" because she was so tiny (and perhaps because she was 10 years his junior), and they married in 1908. Together they had five children, of whom Jean was the third—and one of two girls.

The Ramsays emigrated to the U.S. in 1915 and moved to St. Paul, Minnesota. Louis traveled often as

Ramsay dad and brothers; Louis in the center.

a salesman, going out West and sending postcards of the interesting places he saw. However, he loved being home with his family. In an era when snapshots were not common, they took many candid photos of the family, often with the children climbing all over their dad—or playing dress-up games with their mother. It was a home filled with love and activity. The children made great fun with what was available, and usually the boys included their sister Jean in their activities.

However, one Saturday morning when Jean was nine, she looked out the window to discover that the boys were going off without her. We can imagine how it all happened.

She burst out the front door.

"Wait! Hey, wait for me!" She trailed a distance behind, pulling on her favorite red sweater against the cool morning.

Louis, Robina, and baby Bob.

Nearly halfway down the block already, her brother Bob turned back. "Not today, Jeannie. Go on home. We'll be back soon." He turned and trotted after his brothers.

Determined not to be left out of the fun, Jean followed anyway. If there was an adventure, she'd be a part of it—big brother's blessing or not. As she ran block after block, still able to see them in the distance, Jean wondered where they were going—what kind of fun it would be.

Until she stepped off the curb.

Right into the path of a car. A screech and a thump. That's all there was to it.

The boys, at least a block away, heard the screech—and the shouting that ensued.

"Ambulance! Call for an ambulance!"

Putting off their fun for the moment, the boys backtracked to see what had happened. And in the confusion of the accident, they saw people gathered around a figure on the ground. It was Bob who recognized the little red sweater.

"Jean? Jeannie! That's my sister! Oh, Jean!"

"Step back now. Be careful there, son."

The boys exchanged glances and knew what they had to do. Racing back home, they burst into the kitchen.

"Jean's dead! She got hit by a car, and she's not moving!"

Their mom tore off her apron and their dad quickly slipped into his shoes, but by the time they all ran to the scene, the ambulance had already left. Some bystanders told them that Jean was alive and directed them to the hospital where she'd been taken. They soon learned that she had a serious concussion.

Learning of the accident, some neighbors stopped by the house later that day. They attended the Congregational Church, which called a special service to pray for Jean's recovery. Jean spent at least a week in the hospital, and it was because of the church's prayer service that the Ramsays began attending there. The church emphasized salvation, and the family found a more powerful spiritual experience than anything they had previously known. Jean recovered well from her injuries, but she was always fond of telling people that the incident explained any peculiarities she might have had!

When Jean was about nine, her dad and older brother went to a watch-night service, a late-night service to see in the New Year. During the preaching and prayer, her brother Charlie recognized that he needed to make his own decision to repent of his sins, and he accepted Jesus as his Savior and Lord. Arriving home well after midnight, likely brimming over with excitement, Charlie entered the bedroom Jean shared with her younger sister, Barbara, and nudged her awake to ask her an important question.

"Jean, Jean, wake up!"

Jean, having been sound asleep, struggled to wake up.

"Jean, are you saved?"

"Huh?" hair rumpled with slumber, she awoke and propped herself up on one elbow. "Um . . . what does *saved* mean?"

"If you aren't saved, you won't go to heaven when you die!"

Well, that got Jean's attention. She sat rapt as Charlie proceeded to tell her what she needed to do to be saved: to tell Jesus she was sorry for her sins and ask Him to come into her life. There was no question in her mind about what would happen next, and immediately she received Christ as her Savior.

Not long afterward, the Ramsays attended evangelistic services featuring the well-known Pentecostal evangelist, Dr. Charles Price, who emphasized healing and the baptism of the Holy Spirit and speaking in other tongues. Under Dr. Price's ministry, Louis was healed of stomach issues and a skin condition. When she was nine years old, the Ramsays moved to a new neighborhood in St. Paul and started attending a church of a different denomination: the Church of God. Jean once had a Sunday school teacher there who went to Africa to become a missionary. This teacher made a great impression on Jean, inspiring in her the desire to become a missionary too.

It didn't take her long to start serving others. When Jean was a young teenager, Louis regularly helped out at a skid row mission, and he often took Jean and her younger sister, Barbara, to sing at the services. One of the ministers who helped there, C. C. Beatty, was a dean at North Central Bible Institute (NCBI), a new Bible college in Minneapolis. Jean was close to high school graduation, and her dad wanted to interest her in going to NCBI. She wasn't enthusiastic about the idea because she was prejudiced against their Pentecostal theology; it seemed new and strange to her. However, she decided to give North Central a chance along with several other colleges.

Prayerfully, she wrote the names of the schools on slips of paper and put them into a box. She drew out a slip. NCBI's name came out of the box. She still was not convinced, so she repeated the exercise, praying at great length before drawing a name out this time. Again, out came NCBI.

Still unconvinced, Jean relented. "Okay, I guess I'll go there, but I don't want to," she told her dad.

Reluctantly, she enrolled in the second class of the new college, which was headed up by Reverend Frank J. Lindquist. The classes were held at the church that Reverend Lindquist pastored, the Minneapolis Gospel Tabernacle. Her lack of enthusiasm continued. It wasn't what she had expected. She thought they prayed too long. She even began to think about quitting.

Then one day during their chapel prayer time, Jean felt restless. Just as she peeked through her fingers to see the clock and know how long it would be before they were dismissed, a classmate came alongside and began to pray with her. It wasn't what she was expecting. She felt self-conscious. The other girl encouraged Jean to raise her hands and praise the Lord. Still feeling unsure of herself, she relented. When Jean followed the classmate's leading, something began to change inside her, and she began to pray, to truly seek the Lord. Losing herself in worship, she prayed like never before and in the end received the baptism of the Holy Spirit with the evidence of speaking in tongues. Jean said it seemed that only minutes had passed. In reality, it had been four hours—and she hadn't even been tempted to look at the clock.

Harold began attending NCBI the same year Jean did—1931—and he spotted her immediately. Jean, on the other hand, thought Harold would be a good boyfriend for her younger sister, Barbara. It was against the rules of the college for classmates to date, and—to keep their focus on spiritual things—even *conversations* with the opposite sex were discouraged. However, Harold was the vice president of the missionary officers, and Jean was the secretary, so the two obviously had conversations in that context! Also, the students were allowed to eat lunch together on Fridays, supervised by staff, of course. Harold was handsome and charismatic, and Jean was a young woman with an outgoing personality, a dimpled smile, and an interest in everyone. We can only imagine their first conversations.

School Days

Harold had a friend at school named Elmer Niles. One day, early in his time at North Central, Harold saw Elmer walking down the hall, and he knew there was something different in his countenance.

"Elmer, I can tell by your smile that you've received the baptism in the Holy Spirit! I'm going to receive it too!"

Elmer admitted it was true and encouraged his friend.

That night when Harold went to the service, he took his textbooks for the next day's classes.

One of his teachers, Edmund Stevens, approached him with a smile. "That's a lot of books to be carrying into the prayer service. You're not here to study, are you?"

With all seriousness, Harold replied, "Mr. Stevens, I haven't been baptized in the Holy Spirit yet, but I'm going to receive it! I'm determined to stay all night if necessary—so I brought my books for tomorrow's classes in case it takes all night."

"Harold, good for you! Keep seeking. I'll pray alongside you." Edmund Stevens stayed long into the night and prayed with him until he received the promised infilling of the Holy Spirit. What a celebratory moment it must have been when Harold spoke to Elmer the next day!

In the early days, North Central Bible Institute didn't have dormitories. Harold still lived at home on the farm with chores to keep him busy when he wasn't studying. Many of the female students, including Jean, lived and worked in homes of wealthier families in the city. Jean made 18 cents an hour and got meals at a home where she kept house during the week. Jean's Aunt Lily sold her diamond ring to pay Jean's tuition. She had only two dresses that served as good school clothes, and she alternated between the two.

Considering that this was only two years into the Great Depression, many a student had a similar situation. While Jean obviously would have liked to own more dresses, she knew it wasn't an option, so she gave it little thought on most days. However, one day at school, when Jean was inside a restroom stall, she heard two classmates chatting as they entered the room. Just as they entered, Jean realized that *she* was the topic of conversation.

One girl finished her statement with, "You know, Jean—the girl with the red dress."

Jean's face flushed as red as the dress. She stayed where she was until she knew the girls were gone. No matter. Her small budget didn't allow for any more dresses.

Ministry Opportunities

Jean had a heart for ministry as well as a love for children, and she began helping at the Children's Gospel Mission while she was a student at NCBI. In fact, she was in charge of all the children under five. At one point the class had 30 in that age group. She ran children's services along with Dorotha Dobson, her brother Charlie's girlfriend. A gifted teacher, Jean even gathered the neighborhood kids to teach them on her front steps at her parents' home on weekends.

Beyond her personal volunteer work, each student at NCBI was assigned to at least one "opportunity" a

Band for street service.

week for practical service in gospel work. This could be in singing, speaking, playing an instrument, or testimony. These could take place in mission groups, Bible classes, children's meetings, hospital work, or Sunday school. Some students took part in street meetings in downtown Minneapolis, and Harold played his banjo in a musical group that played for street services.

Several family members were also enrolled at NCBI. Jean's brother Murray Ramsay, Harold's sister Gladys Carlblom, and Dorotha Dobson, who would later marry Charlie Ramsay were freshmen at the time that Harold and Jean were seniors.

Each student was required to be a member of one of the various missionary groups—or bands, as they were called. The bands were Homeland, China, India, Africa, Palestine, South America, and Russia. These bands met once a week on Fridays after lunch. Students studied the lands their bands represented and sent letters to missionaries serving in the field. They also prayed at considerable length for the missionaries and the people of the countries represented.

*Senior class: Harold on far right, back row;
Jean on far right, first row.*

Early picture of Harold and Jean.

A Romance Begins

The yearbook for their senior year at North Central listed nicknames, hobbies, and ambitions for the students. Harold appeared to be the more serious of the two, with a hobby of preaching and ambition to "keep the fire burning." His nickname was "Songbird," as he was often asked to sing solos. Jean's more impish nature was evidenced by her nickname, "Miss Littlebit," her hobby of playing pranks, and her ambition "to grow up" (maybe partly due to her 4-foot 10-inch stature)!

In the last several weeks of their third and final year at North Central, students were allowed to date. By then, sparks had begun to fly between the two, and Jean had long since reconsidered her first thought that Harold would be a good match for her sister. Jean must have been thrilled when Harold lost no time in asking her out, because she immediately agreed. Their first date began with feeding the ducks at Loring Pond. What must have been going through their minds on that day?

"She's such a beautiful girl. Will I seem too forward if I hold her hand?"

"What if he wants to hold my hand? What will I do if he asks to kiss me?"

Whatever their thoughts were, we can imagine their interest in one another likely outweighed that toward the ducks. The same held true later that day as the pair attended a service with evangelist Billy Sunday. Sunday, a fiery preacher who was well known across the country, regularly drew large crowds eager to listen. Both Jean and Harold felt a call into the ministry, and this first date reflected that desire to serve God. But even during Sunday's dynamic preaching, they paid more attention to one another than they did to the speaker.

Years later Jean told of this date, "You won't be surprised when I say that neither of us could tell you anything about the sermon. Well, it was our first date; and after three years of relative silence with each other, perhaps we didn't listen carefully to the evangelist."

The handsome young man with dark wavy hair and the girl with the winning smile and deep dimples no doubt made a striking couple among the others at the service. They had known each other through three years of Bible school, but on this day—their first date, they found each other's company very special; and they knew immediately that this was love!

Jean went on to explain what the pair was able to recall of Billy Sunday's preaching. "One thing we did remember was a story he told about a young couple in love who had a secret code, 143, which stood for a one-letter word, a four-letter word, and a three-letter word, meaning 'I love you.' We picked that right up, as we could use it in the presence of others—and on the phone."

The opportunity for dating was short in those few weeks of their final semester. However, they had come to know each other well during the years of school, and their engagement was announced at the senior class banquet. After graduation, they would strike out in opposite directions to obey God's call on their lives, a call that each of them felt strongly. It was then that the two would see whether their feelings were strong enough to survive the separation.

Chapter 2

Starting in Ministry: The Preparation

*Be very careful, then, how you live—
not as unwise but as wise,
making the most of every opportunity.
—Ephesians 5:15-16*

Soon after graduation, Jean and her friend Ann Ringness headed to Rolette, North Dakota, a small prairie town nearly 500 miles from Minneapolis. The tiny community was surrounded by farm fields. Olga Olson, the pastor there and a former classmate, had invited them. Their job? To facilitate vacation Bible school and do children's ministry. The pay was probably room and board and little else.

Hosted by the pastor, Jean and Ann must have been surprised when they were first led upstairs to their living quarters: an unfinished attic with sparse furnishings. Jean later recalled their response when bad thunderstorms rolled over the prairie. Accompanied by deafening crashes of thunder, the winds threatened to tear away the roof only inches above their heads.

"Huddling under our blankets, we sang 'God Will Take Care of You' at the top of our lungs to drown out the sounds of the storm!"

One day Jean and Ann received word that Pastor Olga was ill. When they went to call on her, she asked them to take over her duties at the church temporarily: preaching, leading the weekly prayer service—everything. It was an unexpected challenge, but it was in the service of the Lord. They handled it and learned something about themselves in the process.

Harold's Ministry

Meanwhile, Harold began traveling with evangelist Virgil Jackson, alternately preaching with him in evangelistic services while Harold also led songs and sang solos in his rich tenor voice. They traveled through Ohio, Indiana, Missouri, Oklahoma, and even into Colorado.

Harold kept up a prolific correspondence with Jean during those months of 1934 into 1935, writing almost daily letters to her. Jean's address in Rolette was Box 143, which was fortuitous in light of their secret code. The envelopes Jean received displayed *Box 143* written very prominently.

One day Jean stopped by the post office looking for her daily letter. The postmaster attended the church where Jean was ministering, so maybe he felt that he could ask a question. Just imagine the conversation:

"Why does your friend write the numbers *143* so big on the envelopes?"

"Oh, it's just a secret meaning," Jean replied airily.

But the postmaster wouldn't let it go. "Truly, in all my years at the post office, Miss, I've never seen any other envelopes with the box number written so large—only yours. It must be something interesting."

Jean's face likely turned a bit pink at that.

And then, cajoling to tease the meaning out her, he continued, "What does it mean?"

Jean relented. After all, it felt wonderful to share it in the end. She told him of Billy Sunday's preaching and the secret code that meant "I love you" delivered daily from someone very special.

Wedding Bells

When winter came, the time at Rolette came to an end, and Jean returned home to Minneapolis. The couple kept up their prolific correspondence while Harold continued in evangelistic work. Harold often wrote poems throughout his life, and undoubtedly Jean received some at this time. The letters from early in the summer after their graduation spoke of a future together obeying God's call on their lives.

Efforts began in earnest to plan their wedding for the spring. Irene Lindquist, Pastor Frank Lindquist's wife, helped Jean to plan a wedding that wouldn't cost a lot in those depression years.

The wedding was held on April 21, 1935, Easter Sunday afternoon, when the church was already decorated with flowers. There was no fancy reception and no invitation costs. There had simply been an oral invitation issued to the congregation. The wedding was sweet

Charlie, Dorotha, Jean, and Harold.

Wedding day.

and simple, a pledging of their lives and love to each other. Harold and Jean's story would be a love story from beginning to end—love for each other and love for God and His work.

The newlyweds caught a ride as far as Chicago with another couple who had just married, John and Ruth Strand. The Strands were heading farther east, and the two couples parted ways, wishing one another all the best.

Very soon after their honeymoon in Chicago, Jean and Harold began their ministry together with services at South Bend, Indiana, in May. Harold contacted pastors he knew from previous ministry to set up special services. From Indiana they went to Lansing, Michigan, for a tent meeting. The newspaper ad read, "Hear the fearless gospel preacher Harold Carlblom of Minneapolis, Minnesota, in the Big Tent on Cady Court." Another flier from Mankato Gospel Tabernacle advertised, "Evangelist Harold Carlblom, a little preacher with a big message."

They purchased a 1931 Chevy coupe to travel to their evangelistic campaigns, which led through Indiana, Michigan, Ohio, Illinois, Wisconsin, and Minnesota during 1935. Their home base was in Minneapolis, where both Jean and Harold's parents were still located.

By November, when churches were not having special services during the holiday season, Harold started work at Dayton's Department Store for the 1935 Christmas season. He kept the job longer than the other seasonal workers, which meant he was present for the birth of their first daughter, Joanne Ruth, on January 18, 1936. Some might have thought the couple would settle down after the baby came—but that

Jean and Harold Carlblom with Ruth and John Strand honeymooning in Chicago.

wasn't the case. Not even close. To give Jean time to recover from Joanne's birth, Harold's sister Lorraine joined him in the services, which started soon afterward in Mankato. When Jean resumed traveling with Harold, it was with baby Joanne in tow.

The couple went on holding revival services throughout the Midwest, with Harold preaching and the two of them singing duets. Jean also played the accordion, while Harold played a tenor banjo. Typically, their campaigns lasted two or three weeks in a church, or even up to a month, with services six nights a week. There were very few breaks between the scheduled services, so it kept them very busy. They held no other jobs, so they depended on the Lord to provide services at churches. Harold always preached with passion and no doubt thrived with this schedule. Apparently, his preaching touched hearts, as they were asked to apply as pastors in at least one of the churches where they ministered; but they didn't feel it to be God's will at that time. Instead, they sometimes filled in for pastors, and they continued holding evangelistic services, sometimes staying with the pastors, sometimes in the spare room of a congregant. No matter what the situation, they were spending time in training for what God was calling them to do.

Months of evangelical meetings came and went, and in 1937 their schedule took them to Wisconsin to the Fond du Lac Gospel Tabernacle. As usual, while they were there, the Carlbloms stayed with a family: the Liebelts. Little did they know that one day their daughter Joanne would be a pastor's wife at that very church—and their yet unborn daughter Marjorie would marry a Liebelt.

At the end of each year, when no special services were scheduled because of the Christmas season, the young family would return to the Twin Cities and stay with the parents of either Harold or Jean. Invariably, Harold was welcomed back to Dayton's for the holiday seasonal employment, usually in the toy department.

During all their years of traveling, Jean kept a scrapbook containing meticulous records of the towns where they held services, the pastors, and with whom they stayed. They made many

Louis, Robina, Grandma Low.

Starting in Ministry: The Preparation   33

friends around the country, friends who would last a lifetime. Several news clippings mention that even three-year-old Joanne sang in the services. While many a young woman would have longed for the permanence of a home she could call her own, Jean seemed content with an itinerant lifestyle as, alongside her husband, she obeyed God's call to ministry.

Pastoring

After nearly five years of travel, God's call would change their ministry. In March 1940, they were unanimously elected to the pastorate in the small town of Burwell, Nebraska,

All the Ramsays. Back row: Louis, Murray, Charlie. Middle row: Barbara, Bob. Front row: Jean, Robina, Grandma Low.

where they had previously held special services. There they held a daily vacation Bible school with an enrollment of 140—fully 10 percent of the town's population—and stirred enough interest to attract a newspaper reporter from nearby Ord, who wrote a report. During their time in Burwell, their second daughter Patsy Jean was born. It was a successful tenure in Burwell but a short one. Believing that God had something different for their ministry, they resigned in June 1941.

Trusting in God's leading, Harold and Jean took a pastorate in Kalispell, Montana, a few months later

Barb, Dode (Harold's youngest sister), and Jean with Patsy and Joanne.

after being unanimously elected once again. Always hard workers, they held special meetings with Christian Hild, an evangelist who traveled widely. Vacation Bible schools and youth rallies also became part of their Kalispell ministry. The Carlbloms enjoyed the beauty of the mountains and lakes in this area, as well as the ministry to people they loved and kept in touch with for many years. However, they left Kalispell in December of 1942 to accept a call to serve as assistant pastors to Rev. J. R. Kline at Berea Tabernacle in Detroit, Michigan.

There must have been a restlessness in Harold to find the spot that God had for his ministry. Just over a year later, in January 1944, the Carlbloms left Detroit to go back into evangelistic work. By that time, Patsy— not quite three—had begun joining big sister Joanne singing in the services and reciting Scripture. At some point, the Carlbloms purchased a 1941 Plymouth travel trailer to make it easier for living conditions for the family, possibly because Harold and Jean were feeling a pull toward missionary service. About this time, Harold inquired with the World Missions Department of the Assemblies of God about ministry in Alaska, which had not yet achieved statehood.

However, in September 1944, they received a call to pastor in Tacoma, Washington, at Glad Tidings Assembly of God. It must have been difficult, having a heart for missions and yet receiving call after call to pastor churches. The Carlbloms continued to trust the Lord's leading. Harold, upfront about feeling a strong call to missions, told the board in Tacoma that he didn't know how long they'd be there. However, the board was agreeable with that and issued an invitation for Harold and Jean to be their pastors until God made it possible for them to go into missions.

During their time pastoring in Washington, the Carlbloms spent time with the families of Ralph Devin and Raymond Busby, both missionaries to Indonesia. Ralph and Raymond, learning of the Carlbloms' desire for mission work, urged Harold and Jean to become missionaries in Indonesia. During the weeks and months of these discussions and amid much prayer for guidance, their third daughter, Marjorie Rae, was born in October 1945 in Tacoma.

Soon afterward, Harold and Jean felt that the moment to take action had come; it was time to obey God in going to the mission field. The family left the Tacoma pastorate in November to prepare for missions. They went into intensive itineration to raise the necessary financial and—just as important—prayer support. Itineration meant travel, for Jean and Harold held missionary services in many of the churches where they had held evangelistic services across the Midwest, as well as their former pastorates in Kalispell and Detroit. Their last service was set for Minnesota. It was announced in a flier for a farewell in December at their home church, the Minneapolis Gospel Tabernacle.

Finally, all the money was raised. The prayer partners

were set. All the plans were laid. And they left for the West Coast for more missionary services there before setting out on the mission itself. The Carlbloms visited California for the first time and saw the redwoods. They took part in a Youth for Christ rally in San Francisco, and a photo of their family singing appeared in the San Francisco Examiner. Jean later said that Patsy, at only five years of age, was "scared stiff" of the flash and almost stopped singing.

While a bright flashbulb might have seemed unusual and frightening for little Patsy, little did she know what else was in store as her family prepared to leave everything familiar.

Chapter 3

Heading for Indonesia

*Your path led through the sea, your way
through the mighty waters,
though your footprints were not seen.* —Psalm 77:19

Finally, the moment of departure arrived, the moment that would change the trajectory of their lives. The *S.S. Monterey* was a large passenger liner of the Matson Line. The twenty-day voyage would take them to Hawaii, Samoa, New Zealand, and finally Australia. There they'd wait for visas to get into Indonesia.

They received a lovely send-off from a dear friend Mary Jane Lanphear, who would later serve as a missionary in Indonesia alongside her husband Leonard. She kindly sent a series of notes for Jean and Harold to

The Carlblom family boarding the ship to leave for Indonesia.

Indonesia

200 miles

JAVA
on a larger scale

100 miles

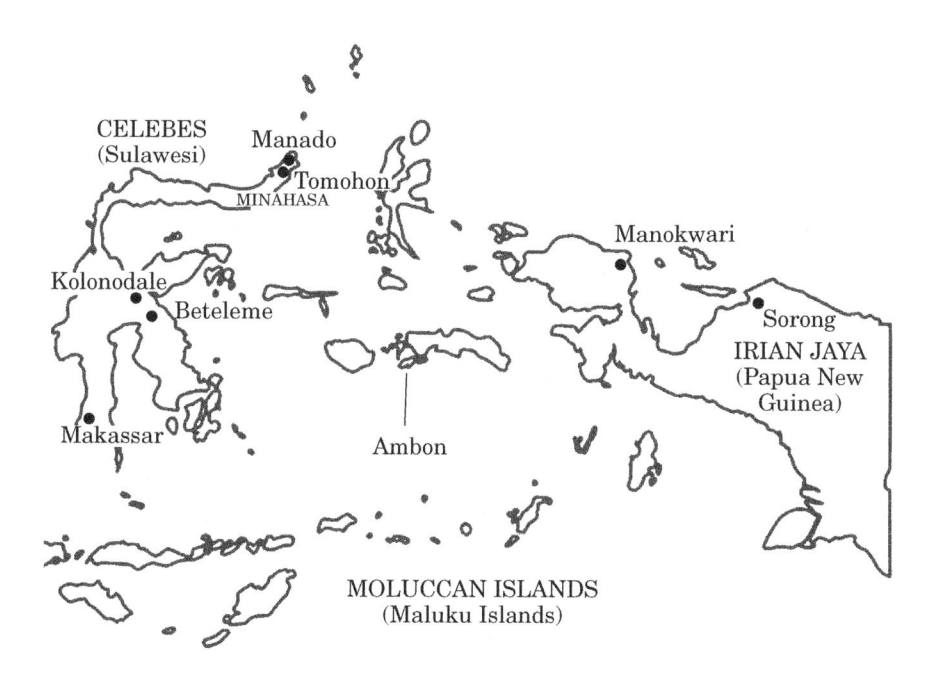

Heading for Indonesia 39

CELEBES (Sulawesi)
Manado
Tomohon
MINAHASA
Manokwari
Kolonodale
Beteleme
Sorong
IRIAN JAYA (Papua New Guinea)
Makassar
Ambon
MOLUCCAN ISLANDS (Maluku Islands)

open and read on their journey. This poem was meant for the sailing day:

> *Five little people, I would say*
> *Are leaving for Aussie Land today*
> *In a great big ship—The Monterey.*
>
> *They are soldiers of the Cross.*
> *They will never suffer loss,*
> *For with Jesus at their side*
> *They will in His love abide.*
>
> *The Lord bless our Carlbloms dear*
> *While they work for Jesus there.*
> *And may precious souls be won to Him*
> *And many rescued from their sin.*
>
> *With you our prayers are sailing, too*
> *That God will bless and keep you true,*
> *That we may soon meet you again*
> *And work for Him unto the end.*

A lovely sentiment it was to set the tone for the trip—a good reminder of the many supporters they were leaving behind, physically—but not in spirit. Thankfully, another missionary couple was also aboard: Kenneth and Gladys Short, and their two sons, David and Donny. They didn't realize it then, but this family would later be important in the Carlbloms' early ministry in Indonesia.

The ocean trip wouldn't be without its challenges. Jean and Harold were assigned the first seating for the dining room on the *Monterey*. In one letter Jean wrote it was "Awful early with kiddies—7:00 a.m. to be all dressed and washed and combed." While rising early for breakfast would be a matter of routine after the first few days, it wasn't the only difficulty. Staterooms are notoriously small—especially for a family of five—and space to live and play was at a premium. Then came the measles outbreak on the ship, and all children aboard were inoculated "on the sit-down place."

Even with the drawbacks, the ship was an exciting place for their young family. None of the family had ever traveled by ship before, so everything was new and exciting for them all. The children anticipated—and also dreaded—the loud ship's horn that sounded when leaving ports. The girls covered their ears, trying to drown out the sound. After they acquired their sea legs, and as long as the weather was fair, the numerous decks allowed the family to walk all around the ship. The sight of the great, wide Pacific Ocean was truly awe-inspiring. Harold and Jean prayed for God's guidance as they anticipated the end of the trip.

While the passage would be lengthy—nearly three weeks—a few stops along the way broke up the monotony. On May seventh, the *Monterey* arrived in Honolulu at 6:00 p.m., and the passengers were delighted by the lively music of a Hawaiian band accompanied by lovely young ladies offering leis—traditional Hawaiian welcome gifts—for the passengers. The Carlbloms went ashore to eat in a restaurant. The next day Harold, Jean, and the girls went shopping and visited Waikiki Beach before heading back to the ship, which sailed at 5:30 p.m. As they embarked, passengers threw their leis, along with coins, into the water, as was the custom with departing travelers. The coin divers quickly retrieved the coins, and soon the ship sailed again.

Another notable happening during the voyage was seeing an active volcano in the distance. What a sight! On May thirteenth the ship docked at Pago Pago in American Samoa. Despite the rain, the Carlblom and

Short families went ashore, where the children received lots of attention from the Samoans. As the Carlbloms chatted with the people, some who spoke English said, "Why don't you stay here? We want missionaries too." But it was not to be. Their plan took them back on the ship after only hours. They soon crossed the International Date Line, skipping a whole day. They went from May 13 straight to May 15.

It was about then that they also experienced a couple days of very rough sailing. It was bad enough struggling to walk on the ever-wavering ship, but then seasickness came. Those days were no fun.

When the ship made port in Auckland, New Zealand, on May 18, Harold and Kenneth Short went to town in the evening and found a Youth for Christ meeting in progress. The men were asked to give their testimonies. The next day was Sunday, and the Carlbloms attended and took part in three different services—morning, afternoon, and evening. The ship sailed again on May 20; with crowds on the dock, thousands of crepe paper streamers flung from the ship's decks created a web as they crisscrossed, fluttering to the dock below.

Finally, on May 23, the *Monterey* arrived in Sydney, Australia, at 10:30 in the morning but spent three hours anchored for inspection before being allowed to dock. Much red tape caused a delay, and the family spent the rest of the day in customs. However, upon arrival in Australia, the Carlbloms acquired a support system. The Busby family, with whom they had spent time in Washington, met them in Sydney along with another family, the Greenwoods, who were pastors in Melbourne. The Busbys were also awaiting re-entry to Indonesia. The Carlbloms still weren't in Indonesia, but they were getting closer!

Even though they'd traveled halfway around the world to get to Indonesia, the family remained in Australia for over three months, awaiting visas. The systems were backlogged with refugees who were returning to Indonesia after World War II. While they waited their turn, Harold, Jean, and the girls stayed near Melbourne in a small cottage on the beach. The most bothersome issue? No indoor plumbing. In the end, this drawback would help prepare them for life in Indonesia. Also, May through August was winter in the Southern Hemisphere, so they had little opportunity to enjoy the wide expanse of beach, although the girls whiled away many hours playing on a nearby swing set.

While they were waiting in Australia, Harold was asked to speak at several nearby churches. Final approval for the visa came in August, and the Carlbloms prepared to set out for the long-awaited final leg of their journey.

Passage to Indonesia was aboard the crowded Dutch evacuee ship, the *Tasman*. The family traveled with about 400 returning refugees from the war, when Indonesia had been occupied by the Japanese. Many were Dutch people returning to Indonesia as well as Australian brides of Dutchmen.

In contrast to their relatively luxurious passage on the *Monterey*, this trip would have little in the way of comfort. First, no cabins were available. Thus, they were assigned to bunks. The wards filled with endless rows of bunks were less than appealing. Not only that, the family couldn't even bunk together. Harold's assignment was in the hold, where the air was hot and stuffy. Jean's assignment was in a ward of 40 beds in rows, along with baby Marjorie and little Patsy. And that left Joanne. At only 10 years old, she was assigned in a similar ward—but all by herself and all the way on the other side of the ship. Privacy did not exist. Neither did service. There was little in the way of conveniences, only small, smelly, filthy public toilets that sometimes had lines of people waiting to use them. Stories circulated of big rats on the *Tasman*, which brought great excitement and dread to the kids. Jean kept a newspaper clipping mentioning the rats on the ship, but thankfully, the family did not see them.

Jean and Harold could have looked on the journey as a precursor of what was to come: trading comforts for discomfort and privacy for a decided lack thereof. The one constant, they knew, was the Lord's presence.

Chapter 4

Arrival and Settling In

Therefore go and make disciples of all nations, baptizing them in the name of the Father and of the Son and of the Holy Spirit, and teaching them to obey everything I have commanded you. —Matthew 28:19-20

September 13, 1946, brought their arrival in Batavia, as Indonesia's capital city was known then, although it would eventually be changed to Djakarta, and later, to Jakarta. Indonesia, formerly the Netherlands East Indies, had declared its independence from the Dutch colonialists on August 17, 1945. For some time the new country worked to establish itself, which was no small task when a nation is made up of over 17,000 islands in an archipelago that stretches across almost 5,000 kilometers between the Indian and Pacific Oceans. Revolutionary struggles continued to arise, and the Dutch government didn't recognize the new country until 1949.

What a new experience it was for the whole family! The humid air was oppressively hot. Batavia was big and noisy and dirty, and various odors (food, exhaust, animals, and their excrement) filled the air. Streets were always busy, overflowing with oxcarts, bicycle-driven mini taxis called *becas,* (pronounced betchas), cars, motor scooters, three-wheeled electric carts, and countless street vendors. Incessant honking of horns added to the clamor.

Some sights seemed so strange to them. Nearly every food vendor balanced a bamboo pole over his shoulders, balancing a little charcoal grill on the end, on which he could grill you some skewered meat called *sate* (pronounced sah-tay) or some other savory treat. Peddlers sold various items from the bamboo poles on their shoulders—maybe baskets or pots and pans. All the vendors would call out the names of their products as they walked up and down the streets, adding to the cacophony.

Ditches along the sidewalk often held stinking raw sewage, as did the large canal that flowed through the middle of the city, contributing to the mélange of odors.

Even being inside a house felt a lot different from anything the Carlbloms had experienced. Little lizards called *tjitjaks* (pronounced chee-chaks) ran up and down the walls and ceilings of homes, which were not anything like the homes back in the States. Built by the Dutch colonials, they had airy transoms to allow for maximum airflow in the tropical heat, but this meant that all the creepy crawlies could find their way in, too.

> *"I can remember being scared to put my feet in my shoes, in case a scorpion was in there!"* —Patsy

Patsy remembers watching the *tjitjaks* crossing the ceiling, and hoping they wouldn't suddenly lose their grip and fall down when they were above her! The warnings to look in their shoes for scorpions before they put them on was no joke either. Plus, in Djakarta there was no shortage of rats like they'd seen on the *Tasman*.

The family was housed in a warehouse space with businesses all around, and the only area for the kids to play was in a dusty alleyway behind the building. Only the overhead transoms and portable fans were available to cool the rooms, so it was hot for sleeping. Mosquito nets were draped over the beds to avoid the dreaded bites that might result in malaria.

They found Indonesian bathrooms to be different and sometimes challenging. Bathrooms in Indonesia are typically two rooms. One is the shower room called the *mandi* where there is a large tub of water, not to get into, but to pour cold water over one's body. Then the bather is supposed to soap up and rinse the soap off, again with cold water, which then runs down the drain in the middle of the floor. Even in a tropical country, the resulting chill will wake a person up!

The toilet is generally in a separate small room called the *kamar kecil*. In European-built homes, it was much like the toilets they knew in the U.S., but with the tank overhead, and the flush released by pulling a chain. In native homes—and quite often in public places—there was a hole in the floor over which to squat to do the necessary business, and the waste was washed away by pouring water down the hole. Toilet paper was very seldom available—instead there was a can of water to wash oneself. One of the few comforts from home was the toilet paper that Jean and Harold had brought along in their storage drums.

"These bathrooms are sure different from the ones in America!" —Patsy

Not long before the family arrived, Ralph and Beryl Busby, pioneer missionaries to Indonesia, had just established a Bible school in Djakarta in order to train nationals to become leaders and pastors in their own country. Though Indonesia is a predominantly Muslim nation, many of the people are animists, believing that inanimate objects have spirits. Often their religion is a mixture of these, and sometimes ancestor worship is mixed in as well.

In the beginning, so they could communicate in their new and strange land, Harold and Jean went through a few months of language training in Djakarta. They learned the Indonesian language, which was the official language of their new country. However, many dialects were spoken in the various islands. At the same time, Joanne and Patsy were enrolled in an Indonesian school—but without speaking a word of Indonesian! It was sink or swim! Interestingly, the girls learned the basics of the Indonesian language more quickly by playing with children at school than their parents did in their own language school.

After language training, the missions leadership in Indonesia decided that the Carlbloms were most needed on the island of Borneo (now named Kalimantan) in the city of Bandjarmasin (now spelled Banjarmasin), which is situated on the confluence of the Barito and Martapura rivers. The missionary family who had been stationed there, Kenneth and Gladys Short, would soon be leaving for Manila to take charge of the Assemblies of God radio station there.

Chapter 5

Bandjarmasin

*For in the day of trouble he will keep me safe in his dwelling;
he will hide me in the shelter of his sacred tent
and set me high upon a rock. —Psalm 27:5*

Street scenes in Bandjarmasin, nicknamed Bandjar, were similar to those in Djakarta on the island of Java, but compared to Djakarta's crowded streets, a much more important part of transportation and commerce happened on the river. The river was muddy and brown, but it was busy. A floating market where many goods and foods were sold took up a good amount of space on

Prow crossing the river.

that river. Some people lived on their boats, sold goods from them, and seldom left them.

Also, many large dugout canoes, sometimes with canopies for relief from the tropical sun, crossed the river regularly to take traffic from one side to the other. The Sunday school was across the river from the Carlblom home, and they often crossed in one of those watercrafts, standing with other passengers, some with bicycles. A canoe ride was much faster than driving many kilometers to a bridge.

Typical river traffic.

Jean regularly wrote her family back in the States to describe the country and their living conditions. She also corresponded with friends and the various churches supporting their missionary endeavors.

Dear Mother, Daddy, Grandma, & Barb, June 1947

There is a nice breeze tonight, and it helps to blow some of the mosquitoes away. I guess Harold told Barbara about our new Sunday school. That's about all we can think of these days, for it surely thrills our hearts. I never realized before how hard it is to begin to bring the gospel to those who have never heard. All they know is ancestor worship and "adat" (custom or tradition). They offer sacrifices—they have altars in every home, and we have not yet learned the meaning of what is on the altar. But you always see large pictures of the departed mother, father, grandparents; and they worship these.

It is not easy to bring the gospel to those who are so blinded. It must be made so very simple. What is salvation—they don't need it perhaps, and who is Christ? There is a God they know of—Muslims have Allah. We have to first show them their need—their sin, and then present Christ as their Savior from the guilt and punishment for sin. I find that most of my object lessons or flannel-board material are meant for American children who understand all these fundamentals. But they are extremely interested. People will not go far to a meeting. Those within a few blocks come, but when they are really saved, or if there is a special hunger, they will go a long way. So we want to start Sunday schools in all districts, and then gradually add services as we are able. Now we are still looking for a place for another Sunday school, but have no funds.

Did I tell you we ordered Story-O-Graph material—$100 worth, and we thought they'd take it out of our fund in Springfield that is from offerings sent in above our support, but they took it out of our check this *month—that is, $26. They plan to take that much out every month, I guess. Well, this month it was all right because the Lord prompted a friend in Detroit (whom we thought had very little) to send us $70. No doubt it was a great sacrifice for her, but oh, what a help it was! God will provide. So far we have gotten along fine—always eat, and we have little need of buying much, so we manage fine. You always ask about our finances, and so we try to explain the situation as best we can.*

Much love, Jean and Harold

The Carlblom home was a typical Dutch-built home. The front part consisted of two adjoining bedrooms off a larger room intended to be a living room, but which was to be used for the church services and the Bible school. These would start as soon as it was feasible. A long veranda to the side lay along several smaller rooms that were used for storerooms and extra bedrooms. At the far back of the house were the toilet and shower rooms, the kitchen, and a bedroom for Inam, the hired cook.

It might seem that missionaries shouldn't be wealthy enough to have a servant, but it's customary in countries like Indonesia, partly because it's so cheap to hire help, and also because it frees the missionaries' time to do what God has called them to do. It's a desirable position, and those whom the Carlbloms hired grew to be like extended family.

The family was concerned about security because of a small canal behind the house near Inam's quarters. Wanting to be sure she was safe, Harold rigged up a crude alarm with a rope that led from the servant's quarters, along the length of the house, and to his and Jean's bedroom. A few tin cans dangled from the rope in their bedroom, so if Inam was frightened of anything, she could signal Jean and Harold by pulling the rope.

We can imagine the chaos one night during a loud storm when the cans went to jingling.

Harold leapt from the bed.

"Jean, check on the girls and stay at this end of the house."

With the wind swirling violently, Harold took charge. Carefully and alertly, searching for the trouble, yet as quickly as possible, he picked his way along the veranda to the back of the house. When he arrived in the kitchen, there it was: evidence of a break-in. He alerted the police quickly, but the intruder had escaped by way of the canal. Thankfully, they were all safe.

Patsy and Inam.

Of course, the neighborhood wasn't all bad. Next door on one side stood a home that was a mirror-image to theirs, where a Chinese doctor and his family resided. The family had four children who often played with the Carlblom girls. To the other side of their home sat a police station, which created a feeling of safety.

However, one night, long after the children had been tucked into bed, they awakened to a strange sight. It's easy to wonder just how the situation played out and what must have been going through their minds.

Their daddy whispered hoarsely, "Jean, lift! Yes, that'll do it. Now hold it there."

"Harold—please! Crouch down. It's safer on the floor."

The girls were confused. Their parents had dragged mattresses into their bedroom and were placing them up against the walls!

"Mommy? Daddy? What—"

It was Jean who whispered first. "Hush, dear. It will be fine. Lie down. Stay there in your bed. There, there. Everything will be fine."

Then came their parents' murmured prayers for protection. "Lord, we ask for your protection for our family and our mission. We thank you that we are in your hands."

In reality, everything was not fine. Guerillas who were fighting against the government had come out of the jungles—and were firing shots at the police station.

> "The possibility of someone shooting at our house was both terrifying and exciting!" —Patsy

Located so close to the station, Jean and Harold tried to guard against stray shots. Eventually the shooting stopped, and all was well. We might wonder now if Harold and Jean questioned their decision to take their young children on the mission field. Even so, it was all quite exciting for the kids!

> Dear Mother and Dad and Barbara,
>
> A plane is going out this morning, so we must rush another letter off, or else it will have to wait a week.
>
> Coming to Borneo was like coming to a new land in some ways. The presence of the rivers and the difference in the houses give it an entirely different aspect. There are not so many on the street, for they also have the rivers for transportation. They use homemade canoes that are longer and wider than ordinary canoes at home, and they are made of black ironwood and are

never painted. Many people live in them with all of their worldly possessions, which perhaps consist of the clothes they wear and a tiny charcoal stove about the size of a pail. They paddle up and down the rivers day after day. At times there is quite a traffic congestion on the smaller rivers. Little children learn to sit quietly in these canoes throughout the day.

Folks travel up inland by river for weeks and weeks to go somewhere. There are stores, restaurants, ferries, and taxis all on the water, but they are all on the same long canoes. A water taxi is longer, with a shade over the center, and is paddled at each end. You really can see how people live as you ride along the river, for many folks build their little thatched huts with the back door over the water and the front leading right onto the street. Many who live like this carry on a business with those on the water and those on the street.

Life is serious for people here. Life is just a struggle to find enough food to exist, I guess. As some of these beggars come to the door with rags of gunny sack clothing or clothing made from the bark of a certain type of inland trees, and we see them full of sores, with little children following them—bony looking and bloated tummies full of disease, I often wonder, "What is there in life for them?" These people never smile, and I think many are worthy beggars. They humble themselves as they beg, dropping to a squatting position which we didn't see them do in Djakarta. The little children trudge door-to-door in the hot sun through the day when you wonder how they walk at all. What joy could there be in a life like this? They beg what they can, steal what they can, and if they are too sick to walk, they lie in the gutter, and no one cares. Oh, how our hearts ache for them! How they need the love of God and the gospel of the Lord Jesus Christ to change their hearts and transform their lives and give them joy and new life. It is all a strange and new story that they cannot understand until they hear it again and again.

We have talked of starting a home and rearing these children for God. The mothers could do the work and be instructed in gardening, and we'd have to get a school teacher, but daily we could give them the Word of God. Pray that God will guide us in this thing and send in the necessary funds and supplies if it is His will.

I wanted to tell you lots more, but the plane is to go soon, and a short letter will be better than none.

Love, Jean and Harold

Before leaving the States, the Carlbloms had packed a number of 50-gallon drums with items they would be needing: toilet paper, bedding, clothing, and canned food. Many cake mixes and pudding mixes had been canned by Women's Missionary Councils at the churches back home. Rice was readily available in the country, as well as fresh vegetables and meat; but they also liked sweet treats, which were not available in Indonesia. While sugar was available, it was coarse and did not work well in American recipes.

"I remember one night when my sisters and I were supposed to be asleep, when I heard my parents buy from the sate *man, and I longed to get up and join them, but I was supposed to be asleep! I could almost taste the goodness of that savory treat!"* —Patsy

Although they were able to have a few familiar comforts, life was markedly different in this new place. Their neighborhood was less busy than in Djakarta, but busy still. Often a barber would set up shop across the street under a tree. Bicycle traffic was continuous, and many others simply walked to their destinations. Occasionally a cart drawn by an ox would roll by. Vendors went up and down the streets, selling their wares. A favorite of theirs was the *sate* vendor. Skewered chicken or beef would be cooked to perfection on the little charcoal grill carried at one end of the pole, then served with a delicious peanut sauce.

> *Dear Mother & Daddy & Grandma,   1947*
>
> *Here we are in a prow—a native home-built canoe. We are two days up inland, which is in the terms of people here—never miles, but how many hours' or days' journey. Our motorboat got stuck in the mud during low tide, so we could not proceed farther in it, as the water kept going down. Fortunately, we were able to hire a prow to take us on up to the village of Pulang Pisau, where Kenneth and Gladys Short worked for about two years before the war. We began about 9:00 Monday morning, and took Joanne, Patsy, and David Short along. It was very hard to say goodbye to Donny (Short) and our Margie, but they were so happy to be going to market with the cook, Inam. We would have felt more at ease leaving the kiddies with friends like at home, but here one doesn't get well enough acquainted with the Dutch. But there is the Chinese doctor next door and he said he'd keep an eye on them, so we went feeling God was leading us on this trip. You see, Shorts had a motorboat that is taken over by the government. Do pray with us that we can get it back. So, because of that we asked if we could get one of the government boats or use Shorts' to go inland. Our purpose was to be introduced and contact these folks before Shorts leave, and tell them of our plans for a Bible school. We prayed God would direct, and if it were His will, to help us get a boat, which He did.*
>
> *There is quite a little preparation, for we can plan on nothing to buy inland. We took a jug of boiled water besides our large teakettle full. We must take all our food, so we planned all meals. We bought a little pressure stove, took lamps, flashlights, dishes, pans, mattresses, and nettings, besides clothes. We left at 9:00 a.m. and traveled maybe half an hour on two small*

*city rivers before reaching the largest river of Borneo—
the Barito. After an hour on this river, which is very
large and beautiful, we entered the canal called the
Anger. We must enter this when the tide is high, otherwise it is dry or almost dry. This is quite narrow, like a
good-sized highway—very beautiful with water palms
(low) growing along the edge, and all sorts of jungle
brush and growth right to the water's edge. We traveled this more slowly, so it takes a little time. We had
a light lunch in the boat, which was just the right size
to accommodate seven or eight. The back part of the
boat has a cover over it, but the sides are all open, with
canvas curtains in case of rain.*

*We got in sight of our first stop about 4:00 p.m., Kuala
Kapuas. We couldn't go on until the next tide to make
the next canal. Just then our motorboat broke down,
and it took us two hours before we arrived, when it
might have been 15 minutes. After working on the boat
all that time a water taxi came along and towed us
the rest of the way in. There is a church in K.K., but it
has run down without care. They wanted us to have
a service, but it was 6:00 p.m. when we arrived, and
with beds to fix up and supper to prepare—Well, we
were invited out for rice dinner consisting of rice and
only meat over it—pork cooked three ways, along with*

The Ambassador, *the motorboat used to go inland
on the river.*

The Sunday school the Carlbloms started in Bandjarmasin.

ketchup (soy sauce). The meat is always so different from ours. They use several ketchup sauces, which give it an entirely different flavor, and often they use their coarse sugar and nutmeg.

We put the kiddies to bed. We thought we'd be in a home, but they had an empty store (small), and we slept there. Harold and I slept on camp cots without mattresses. We really got cold. This climate is strange— so hot, yet at times so cool. I guess one feels the cold much more quickly after being in the heat. We used one double bed netting over our two camp cots, and Shorts also over their two single mattresses. Joanne, Pat, and David slept together. We were all in one room. In the morning we rose and had breakfast with the same folks. Breakfast was only tea—sweet tea. Pat & Jo liked it, but wanted more, which we gave them later.

We left about 9:00 a.m. and traveled the big river Kapuas for a while, and then turned in the canal, but immediately saw the tide was going down. Our boat rides deep so we knew we'd never make it, for the middle of the canal is the shallowest. So when we got in the middle, we began dragging bottom and finally stuck; and it was pouring rain. There wasn't room to put up nets and sleep all night there in the boat, although we could have all sat up under one net if need be. But we began to question prows that passed to see if one would take us on. These prows are quite long, and have a man paddling at each end. We finally found one and transferred all our baggage. The kiddies sat on bedding and the men on suitcases, and Gladys and I sat on the floor, and off we went. In about one and a half hours, we were there at Pulang Pisau, where the canal joins the large river Kahaian. They invited us to sleep in a home where the two rooms had not much division, and very little privacy. We would all be in one room, and their household would be in the other. (The household consisted of well over a dozen, I believe.) So many families live together; sons and daughters and all their children.

Then the man suddenly thought of another place, which was our choice—an empty store again. We had a little over an hour to bathe and get up nets and beds and eat, so we let eating go. We went down to the landing to the little house to bathe. Let me explain. The landing is like a dock, and here they are very long, because of the variances the tide causes. The raft or landing at the end of the dock is floating, and because the tide was low, the ramp slanted down to the water. The women wash clothes on this floating landing, and also there is a little room on it. This has only a floor with a hole in it. It has a double purpose, and we are now to take our bath. We lower our dipper through the hole and get our water, soap ourselves all over, then dip down for dipper after dipper of this dirty water to rinse. Afterwards we go back up to the house and get dressed for the church meeting held in a schoolhouse. I wish I could help you picture these villages inland.

The villages have one path in front of the houses between them and the river, and jungle behind them. The houses are side by side, stretching blocks or even miles up the river, depending on the size of the "kampung" [village]. This path is only a few yards wide, and looks beautiful with palms bending over it, tropical trees shading it, and banana trees placed here and there along the edge of the path. As we walked along, we looked up through the branches of the towering palms silhouetted against the bright sky and saw a full moon shining down on us. Before long we reached the school and found quite a crowd there already. It had been seven years since they had a white missionary there, and they seemed so happy to see us. God blessed, and if no one else's hearts were moved, we know ours were. We have seen and felt the need, but we have no permits for working inland yet. There's no boat and no worker to take our place in Bandjarmasin and no native Bible student to leave in the villages to carry on when we would have to leave. So you see, we have a great deal to do yet.

We came home in a prow, for it's quite a little walk. It was beautiful, with a full moon, big wide river, little dim lights here and there along the shore, the only sound the regular dip of the paddle in the water and the gentle splash it made each time.

Suddenly we heard more—a sound of voices talking in a loud sing-song tone—then we saw flashlights and could see individuals dancing alone very gracefully but oddly. It proved to be right next to where we stay, so we walked slowly up the landing to see all we could see. It was some entertainers from another village—two women and one man—and as they danced slowly around a little box table, they sang to each other. A crowd stood around dropping coins in a container. We could not get the story because we didn't know the dialect—perhaps Dayak (a tribe of Borneo). Then from the other side we heard drumbeats and chanting as Muslims prayed. During the night we were awakened by the drumming and native instruments and strange chanting. This could have been the Muslims, or perhaps the ceremonies following a death. These ceremonies are carried on for maybe a month or two after a death.

However, the greatest disturbances during the night were the rats that seemed to be running races across the floor we slept on. Nevertheless, we awakened rested. We had to leave early the next morning—the motorboat came in on high tide, and we left immediately. We made it fine this time, reaching Kuala Kapuas at 1:00 p.m., and having time for a nap. Then we walked up the village path with a stream of kiddies following us as in the other village. We had a service again that night and went home again the next day. We were so happy to see Marjorie! (She had been left behind with Inam.)

Jean

Not long after arriving, perhaps in three or four months, The Carlbloms were able to start a Bible school in their home, with the help of Kenneth Short. This Bible school was to prepare adult students for the ministry, and there were maybe a dozen students. Hartimedes Pahu was one of the students, and he became Harold's right-hand man, helping him with the ministry Harold continued up the river.

Besides having a Bible school in the living room, the children were exposed to many unusual things. For example, because the family next door was Chinese, during the Chinese New Year celebration, the traditional lion dance was performed in the driveway shared by the two houses. The lion consisted of several men under a colorful costume that included a large, scary lion's head. the costumed beast writhed and danced around while the drums beat steadily with increasing volume. Most of the family were fascinated by the colors, the rhythm, and the spectacle of it all, but little Marjorie

"Hartimedes was my favorite of the Bible school students. He would tease my sisters and me, and he always had a smile and a laugh!" —Patsy

Marjorie, held by Hartimedes, one of the Bible school students, with a pet monkey in the foreground.

was terrified by the lion and the throbbing drums and the shouts that accompanied it all. She ran and hid somewhere in the house till all the commotion was over.

One occasional sight in the neighborhood that Marjorie and her older sisters all loved was a pet orangutan. Orangutans are native to Borneo, and their name comes from *orang hutan*, which means "person of the forest." This orangutan belonged to a banker's family in Bandjarmasin. One of the family's servants seemed to be assigned to the orangutan, as they often saw her carrying it

Carlblom family in 1947

around. Sometimes after the family had entertained guests outside for beverages and snacks, they saw the ape approach the just-vacated table and make its rounds to drain all the glasses—and even the beer bottles!

Both Joanne and Patsy attended a year of Dutch school in Bandjarmasin, immersing them into the culture and helping them quickly learn the Dutch language, which was still widely spoken in Indonesia. The school day ended by late morning, and Jean also taught them at home in the afternoon using Calvert Correspondence School curriculum. Jean never told them that most students got summer vacations, so they finished their grades quickly!

During their time in Borneo, Jean and Harold's fourth daughter was born. Charlaine Kay made her appearance on November 5, 1948, but expectations had been that she would arrive well before that. Jean wrote her grandma Low about it on September thirtieth.

Dear Grandma,

I am already in the hospital—nothing to do but wait, so will write. I am sorry I can't tell you yet if we have a boy or girl, but you perhaps know already (from a telegram). You see, the baby isn't here yet. The doctor says it is time, and it is getting too big, so he is wanting to bring it now. We are not sure of the date. He is sure it is more than eight months. I never have had swelling before, but my feet and legs have been terribly swollen the last four days or so. It's too bad for Harold right now—wanting to visit me and be with me at this time, but Harold Skoog (a new missionary) has just gone to Djakarta, so he has all the services as well as teaching of the girls. (I guess Patsy will have vacation from her courses.) I am glad he doesn't have cooking, cleaning, washing dishes, washing, and ironing—only to direct it.

Grandma, I wish you could see this hospital. A little bit ago a "djongas" (hired man) was sitting on the porch outside the room cleaning silverware with a little piece of dirty cloth and some fine black dirt! Wonder if they'll be sterilized or boiled before I use them. And the dirt here is a heap dirtier than the dirt at home! Usually they use the finest part of ashes for a cleanser for pots and pans.

The hospital here takes up an awful lot of space. It is built so that every room is an outside room, to be cooler. The babies' baskets are in your room or on the porch just outside your room. So you can see them most of the time, except their bathing and changing times. We have tried to get permission to distribute tracts here, but it is run by Indonesians; and due to the political situation, and with so many Muslims, they won't permit it. I have the Dayak (local tribe) nurses help me learn the meaning of words in my Malay Bible, and it may give opportunities to testify.

This section of the hospital where I am is very hot—it does not get the breeze if there is one. I have been walking around to see what I can see, since I don't have to be in bed. I saw them washing dishes—don't think they use hot water, Gram! But generally speaking it seems fairly clean. All plain wooden floors and beds, unpainted. My sheets look clean.

Brother Ralph Devin (another one of the pioneer missionaries to Indonesia) approached us with a suggestion to move to the Celebes [now called Sulawesi], near Manado at the northern tip. It is mountainous and cool there, right near the ocean, a nice city. The work would not be evangelistic or pastoral, but administrative: overseeing some 15 works in that area, advising and instructing the workers, also preaching, giving suggestions for Sunday school work, etc. The works being close would give me opportunity to go along with Harold. Then too, he suggested helping in his Bible school which he hopes to open in January. We do not mean to run away from here, but it seems so tight and *closed—not a chance in these two years for a building or a lot, and nothing has opened up. Kenny Short was here a year before us—two years ago this month.*

Our lease is up in our Sunday school in January, and that cuts out Sunday school and Saturday night service. Even meetings in homes are difficult, for so many live in one house that there is always someone to object. So, we have felt that one (missionary) family is sufficient until things loosen up. And Skoogs didn't want to move, but now their family is going home, and he may move elsewhere, so that leaves us here. Also, if the motor for the boat hadn't been sent yet, we were going to cancel it, but got a letter today that it has been sent, so God must have something for us.

This is my fifth day in the hospital—no baby yet— occasional very slight pains. The doctor said he has used this method of starting things on 300 women in Holland, and only three out of 100 did not respond; 50% responded by the third day, and 50% on the fourth. He gave oil, pills, injection. I had very slight pains a day and night, then stopped—have been in the labor room twice. He tried to reach the water bag to break it. Now he says we can do nothing but wait. He was afraid to wait longer, lest it wouldn't come and he'd have to operate. But God can overrule these things. We are not afraid. Maybe God has a purpose in my being here longer, getting better acquainted to better witness.

Baby Charlaine finally arrived, to the delight of her sisters and her parents, with both Jean and the baby healthy. She received lots of attention from the family, the hired help, and the people from the Sunday school and church.

Dear Family, *January 1949*

The month of fasting of the Muslims (Ramadan) has just passed. We heard their chanting and their cries and beating of the drum often in the stillness of the night. Many times we passed the prayer house or Mesdjid, and have seen them all squatting on the floor chanting in Arabic in unison in reply to the leader. Some of the chanting is very soft and then they increase in volume until their shouts can be heard for blocks. At this time they rise to their feet and lift their hands, bow, then are very silent for a few moments, and suddenly burst out in more shouts. Then they may kneel and bow to the floor. If these shouts arose from the inward joy of sins being forgiven, we would say, "Amen," but the poor souls don't even understand the Arabic they have memorized, and neither do the leaders. They never have services like ours, but faithfully every evening at sundown they answer the call of the drum, and come to pray only a short while. During the month of fasting the women may attend also (the only time), only they remain in a side room and only watch. They do not partake in worship. During the fast they not only fast but feast, too. They refrain from food all day 6:00 a.m.–6.00 p.m., and at night they begin to feast at 6:00 p.m., then pray, then feast all night. We have seen them carry cakes and food of all sorts to the prayer houses. Well, we certainly have witnessed the emptiness of such a worship, and it stirs our hearts to carry the gospel to them at any cost. They are most difficult to reach, but not impossible. We find it extremely difficult to rent places for services, and have not funds to buy or build, so cannot expand as we'd like. But we thank God for the Sunday school He has given us; 150 hungry little souls crowd in every Sunday, and several grown-ups have come to know Christ through these meetings—maybe more than we know.

Love,

Jean and Harold

As 1949 progressed, the family began to look toward furlough, and Jean and Harold decided that Joanne would return to the States before the rest of the family in order to start public school at the beginning of the fall term. She would return to the U.S. with other missionaries who were heading back, stay with Jean's parents, and the rest of the family would follow later. It was only a couple of months, but the whole family missed her presence. Patsy really missed having Joanne to share her bed. Jean wrote that Patsy, then eight years old, surrounded herself with pillows to feel safe!

Heading Home to the U.S.

The family left Indonesia in late October 1949 aboard the Dutch freighter, M.S. Weltevreden. If Harold and Jean had known that the meaning of the ship's name meant "well-pleased," it would have had special meaning, as it would reflect on their heavenly Father's appraisal of their work. The first port of call was Sumatra, one of the large islands of Indonesia. It's situated off the northwestern tip of Java near the Malay Peninsula.

Trips aboard the freighters were long because of the stops to deliver or take on cargo, but the cost was low in comparison to airline flights in those years. Most freighters had about a dozen passenger cabins, and the dining room was where the captain and his officers ate, so the meals were very good. Sometimes passengers would even get to sit at the captain's table—a special honor.

Their next port was Singapore, followed by Penang, Malaysia. These ports were similar to Indonesian ports, and the people spoke Malay, which is closely related to the Indonesian language. Familiarity with the language was a great benefit, for typically the ship would be at a port for a day or two loading or unloading cargo, which allowed the family time to sightsee for a day.

Ceylon was another stop on this voyage, and the family enjoyed dinner at a hotel on the coast and an afternoon watching the breakers crash on the shore. Even though Indonesia is made up of islands in the ocean, the sea is not usually wild and stormy because the many islands interrupt and slow the currents. Ceylon, though, sits at the southern tip of India, with no islands holding back the Indian Ocean south of it. The children were especially impressed by the wildness of the waves crashing on the rocks.

The next port was Djibouti, which was part of French Somaliland at the time. The family got a photo-op sitting atop camels, which was fun for the kids!

The ship proceeded to Suez, and then through the Suez Canal. As they progressed through the Canal at a slow pace, vendors from the surrounding area boarded the ship to sell their wares and then disembarked at the end of the Canal. One of the exotic products being sold? Fried grasshoppers. Patsy absolutely refused to try them!

At the end of the Suez Canal they stopped at Port Said, in Egypt. Finally began the longest leg of the trip, crossing the Atlantic.

Storms were an expected part of these ocean voyages, and because the freighter was a smaller ship, the rough water affected it more than it would a larger vessel. In the dining room, ledges around the edges of the tables kept

"I remember looking across the cabin at the porthole and seeing only sky, and then the roll would take the ship the other way, and all I could see was an angry ocean! I prayed a lot, especially when I was going to sleep at night!" —Patsy

things from falling off—most of the time. Sometimes most of the adults took to their cabins with seasickness, but the children didn't seem bothered. What was scary for the kids was when the ship rolled in the waves.

This ocean trip marked both Charlaine's first birthday and her first steps. Another memorable thing was the ship's library. Each afternoon—when the weather was fine—the steward served soft drinks for the passengers in the library. Patsy loved the bubbly carbonation of ice-cold Pepsi, something she had never tasted before.

After a seven-week voyage, the Carlblom family arrived back in the States. That first night in the U.S., November 30, 1949, the family got a hotel room in Galveston, Texas. It didn't take long to spot a drug store across the street. At that time, finding a drug store meant something important: a soda fountain!

"Let's go get a malt!" Harold made the suggestion first.

The unanimous cheer went up with that suggestion, and for the first time in four years they all walked across the street for malted milks.

The next morning dawned in their home country. Anticipation was high. The Carlbloms boarded the train heading to Springfield, Missouri, to connect with the Foreign Missions Department. After several exciting days in Springfield, they started for Minneapolis. They would be home! Excitement bubbled over at the prospect of being reunited with Joanne and with Harold and Jean's parents. As they neared Minnesota, snowscapes appeared out the train window. How exciting it was—especially for the kids! Two of them had never seen snow!

One of the first happenings in Minneapolis was enrolling Patsy in public school. Though she had finished fourth grade in her correspondence courses and passed the tests with flying colors, it was felt that because she was only eight years old, it would be best for her to be placed in a fourth-grade class in the U.S.

The year back in the States was brimming full with itinerating, visiting various churches that supported the Carlbloms' missionary efforts. After the school year was finished, the whole family was involved in the services. They all wore traditional Indonesian dress and participated by singing together and performing a skit. Music had always been important in the family, and Jean had already taught the girls to harmonize.

The family traveled by automobile all the way to the West Coast to tell congregations about what they'd been accomplishing on the mission field. The car trips were long, but the girls made fun by playing "alphabet" or counting cows. Harold played along, as he loved to identify the different kinds of cattle along the way, harking back to his farm background.

Chapter 6

Bandjarmasin Again: Second Term

But you are a chosen people, a royal priesthood, a holy nation, God's special possession, that you may declare the praises of him who called you out of darkness into his wonderful light. —1 Peter 2:9

Dear Grandma,   December 2, 1950, South Pacific

Yes, we are in the South Pacific already. Isn't that a surprise to you? We were scheduled to go to Japan first from Vancouver, which wouldn't have taken us into the South Pacific. Well, we had a little bit of trouble. We were loaded quite heavily. The last load was lumber, and that was loaded right on top of the deck, part over the hold—or rather around it. We ran into a storm on Wednesday afternoon, and oh, how we rolled and took the beating of the sea all the rest of that day and next night. No one slept that night, for we rolled terribly, almost out of bed—had to wedge ourselves in with pillows and coats and things . . . and all of the passengers seemed concerned about the top-heavy feeling of the ship. The waves dashed clear up on all decks and even broke away an iron rail, and several places bent iron deck rails. Some of the lumber was broken off and consequently loosened the rest of the cargo.

So the next day, even when the wind began to die down we still rolled. They were inspecting it all, of course, and found the whole load of cargo had shifted several feet to one side, so the ship listed to one side. So then they had to take a different course and get out of that wind and storm, as they said the ship couldn't take another night of that without losing her cargo. That would be bad if we lost on one side and we got heavy on the other side. So they are heading for Honolulu, where we will be on Sunday afternoon or night, and we will have to have the cargo changed or corrected somehow. It will take from one to four days, depending on how much they find they will have to do. So we stop at an extra port. That will be interesting, too, even though we have been there before, but of course it makes us longer than planned, too. So instead of getting to Java the twentieth of December, it would be closer to Christmas day or later. Then in talking with the captain, he said it would be later, because our stops in these Japanese ports were going to be more than one day. So now it looks like we may have Christmas in Hong Kong, or else between Hong Kong and Saigon. But they have promised us a tree, and they will perhaps make it nice, because they did all they could do to make it nice at Thanksgiving for the kiddies especially.

On Thanksgiving, which was in Vancouver, they decorated the tables with napkins with turkeys on them, and our table was the only one of the five with a stand-up turkey on it. Then they had nuts and candies, too.

So we will be getting into tropical weather tomorrow—it is already warmer, and then after leaving Honolulu we will get into the cold again. But they just had to reload, so it will be better sailing. You see, we are in calm seas even now and yet we roll terrifically—very smoothly, but yet we lean far to each side and always more to one side than the other. It scares you almost. So if we hit a storm like this we could never take it. And they say we will get into rougher weather again.

Lots of love to all, and we wish you a very nice Christmas with the blessing of the Lord especially on you, Grandma. We love you a lot—you should hear the kiddies tell about their great-grandma. "She's so nice," Pat says, "and she doesn't look old at all. She dresses so nice all the time and is just awfully nice." She remembers your stories, Grandma.

Great-grandma Low was an old-fashioned kind of grandma—soft and warm with a hug that enveloped, and a halo of soft, white hair surrounding her kind face with twinkling blue eyes. She always seemed to have a smile on her face. She was also a bit of a germaphobe, and Jean later would gently tease her grandma with tales of the less-than-clean situations in the mission field.

The Carlbloms reached Indonesia in the first days of 1951, but there was some discussion about where they should go. They arrived in Djakarta and went up to Bogor, in the mountains, while they awaited directions from the missions board. Political unrest permeated the land, and danger lurked in some areas of the country. It was an uncertain time to be returning to Indonesia for mission work.

While waiting in Bogor, Harold spent much time trying to get their belongings through customs. The family stayed there with the Lanphears, Mary Jane and Len, and their sons, Jerry and Gary. The slow progress of all that was wearing on them, along with the indecision of where they'd be going. In addition to that, they had brought a car from the States, and Harold was trying to get it through customs. He told Jean that under the new government ruling, they could pay four times the cost of the car. Harold had more than a little impatience in his nature, and the slow pace of getting their belongings through customs was difficult for him, but looking back he might have said this situation was part of God's refining process.

January 22, 1951, Bogor, Java
Dear Mother and Dad,

We arrived last Tuesday morning—early morning, but they didn't dock, so it was some time before we got ashore. But now we find that we can't get a boat to Borneo until Feb. ninth or so. We never thought it would be that long a wait.

Harold has been down to Djakarta every day since we came. They take a 6:00 o'clock train in the morning and get back at 6:00 at night. The government wants to charge two and a half times the value of the car, plus freight, etc. So we are doing all we can, and praying much. They tell us that, since this new law is in effect, there has been no exception made. So next Thursday we will know, and if they let it through it will be just the Lord's doing. We don't know about the rest of our baggage yet, but Harold went to take that through customs today, and he isn't back yet. Sometimes we think maybe we brought too much with us, for things seem to be so unsettled here. We hear of trouble everywhere. When we were in Hong Kong, the missionaries said everyone told them they were sitting on a time bomb; then in Singapore things were bad, but officials there were telling us that it was bad but not as bad as Indonesia. We haven't heard any shooting, but I guess that isn't all that could happen. The missionaries seem to feel it is best for two missionary couples to be together. Wish we could have someone with us.

Since we were not at the conference, they didn't feel they could make any decision for us, so decided we could go back to Borneo if we wanted. Pray much that we will know what to do. We surely want to be in God's will.

Some talk has been that we go to Manado with the Lanphears—that is the place that Devin has spoken to us about before, though we haven't had a chance to speak with him yet. But someone else may go there after all—maybe the Lord wants the Lanphears and us both in Borneo. May God have His way. We just can't develop much with only one couple. Bro. Osgood said he wouldn't recommend any family coming out again here while the political situation is as it is. We have heard that the water situation is bad in Borneo, and also the food problem—a shortage. However, there is lots here in Java—more than before. You can get almost anything canned, and it isn't too awfully high for some things, considering the good exchange rate. Bro. Osgood feels if another missionary family came out who haven't been here before, they might get scared at the situation and go right back home for the safety of the children.

You heard that John Tinsman and R. B. Cavaness from Ambon got out and are home (the U.S.) now. There are two missionary families here now that are new, but they won't send any more. Right now there are lots of missionaries around. Brother Devin is here with his boat (the Evangel). Thalia, his daughter is here waiting for a new baby—her husband was the pilot on the boat. Morris, their son who is single, is here too, and their little boy Jojo, 8 yrs old. McCombers have 2 kiddies. Lanphears are here in Bogor, and now us. Must stop now—barrels through customs free of customs—Praise the Lord!

Lots of love,

Jean and Harold

The decision was finally made; Bandjarmasin it was. Harold flew to Bandjar while Jean and the kids followed two weeks later by the *Evangel*, the small ship that had been purchased by the Assemblies of God for missionaries' transportation from island to island. While Harold waited for the family to arrive, he wrote to the folks at home. His writing a letter was rather a rarity, as most of his writing had to do with missionary reports; he usually left the newsy letters for the family up to Jean.

February 9, 1951
Dear Mother, Dad, Barb, and Grandma,

Greetings from Harold in Borneo!

I arrived here Tuesday the sixth after spending from January sixteenth till February fifth trying to get everything in readiness there with customs and other offices. You who live in America can't possibly feature spending every day but Sundays and one Saturday going from office to office, here and there, trying to take care of these matters. There is bureaucracy in America, but far more in these places. Well, after three weeks I thought I had everything ready, went to the shipping agent, and he promised to get our baggage on a ship leaving there today for Bandjarmasin, but just this evening I got a wire telling me that it didn't get on!! So now we wait till the end of February for our stuff to arrive, if it does then. Now there won't be anyone of us there to see to it that it gets on, so . . . who knows. It is Speed Trading Company, in whose storeroom we lived when we came in '46, that failed in this. I've had experience with them before where they haven't been efficient. I thought I had learned my lesson.

Well, now to get on with something that I can tell you about Bandjarmasin. The political situation isn't too bad, although there is shooting on the outskirts at night—at least they say so, but I haven't heard anything scary. Oh, there have been several times when it sounded like a shot, but I couldn't say for sure whether it was or not.

I went out this afternoon to do some drumming up for the Sunday school (for children). It has been recessed for several months, so I felt I must get out and do a little advertising. The response was very good, and I am hoping for a good turnout tomorrow afternoon. I will take the little portable organ over there with me. I'll have to hire a little boat to take it down to the Sunday school. I spent a good deal of time on the organ today, too, for this damp climate swells some little pegs under the keys, and when pushed down they won't come back up. Then you have half a dozen or more notes playing at the same time and they won't stop. So I took it apart and sunned it and sandpapered the pegs, too. When carrying it back in the house, I strained my back. It was pretty painful for a while, but the Lord has touched it and it's not so bad now. By the way, if the Sunday school there has any of those small cards or colored pictures, we will always be in the market to receive them. I scoured the place today to get enough together to give out tomorrow. I promised a picture to all who come, and they seemed tickled. I'm really expecting the place to be filled tomorrow.

The church group is pretty small now. We used to have a good number coming, but there are only about a dozen left, the way it looks. It's too bad. So it's the same as starting from the bottom again. However, in spite of the discouragements, I am happy to be here, and looking to the Lord to do a wonderful work for His glory. If only we could get a better place for a church—perhaps across the river. Pray with us to this end. I'm sure the Lord is able to do it if it is His will.

I have a cook and servant girl here now, so I'll be ready for Jean coming next week when she and the family come on the Evangel. Ralph Devin is bringing them, as he is en route to Ambon. Mary Jane Lanphear may come here for a time while Leonard goes to look over the field in Celebes, where they will perhaps move. If not there, they'll be with us. Now I'll sign off for this time. I love ya' all lots and lots and wish I could give you all a big hug and some kisses.

Bye!

Harold

In a form letter Harold wrote to be sent to all their supporters, he said that the political situation was still in an unsettled state, and everywhere he could see military men bristling with guns. Just that morning two columns of soldiers in steel helmets had come down either side of the street, and when a command was given, they all broke formation and went for the nearest tree or shelter, falling on the ground with rifles poised for action. It was practice, of course, but it made the observer realize that at any time it could be real. Shooting went on at night outside the city, and bodies were frequently found floating down the river, hands tied behind them, terribly mutilated. Harold was told that it wasn't safe to go up the rivers, for there were so many bandits.

The Lanphears and Jean arrived, and they all began to try to build up the Sunday school and church, even though plans were still uncertain. Peter Uren, a missionary from New Zealand, was stationed upriver and did not seem to take an interest in the work in Bandjarmasin. A close friendship developed between Jean and Mary Jane, who was suffering some depression and wanted to go back to the States. Mrs. Uren was also living with them, as she was close to the birth of her baby. When her husband brought her down from upriver, he had others with him, and at one point there were 18 people in the house for sleeping.

In April, Harold and Len Lanphear went to investigate ministry opportunities in Minahasa, a region on the island of Sulawesi, and on April 20, Jean and Mary Jane got a telegram saying, "Start packing!" The women immediately began preparations. They would go to Minahasa, on the northern tip of Sulawesi, to the town of Tomohon. Once again, they would go by way of the *Evangel*. What a blessing it was to have their own small ship to transport missionary families from one island to another.

Their new assignment included working with some fellowships that were leaving a different Pentecostal association to join the Assemblies of God. They would also start a church and a Bible school in Tomohon.

Minahasa

The two families left Bandjarmasin on the Evangel. The ship went up the Martapura River to the much wider Barito River, which led to the sea. Both rivers were muddy and brown—and known to contain crocodiles. Captain Ralph Devin had to anchor in the river for several days while they waited for some supplies for the ship.

Tomohon, in Minahasa, was quite different from Bandjarmasin. The new (to them) Carlblom house was built on a hill, on stilts in the front, with a room rather like a basement underneath. When looking out the windows of the front room on that second level, they had clear views of the street and could see students walking to school, the horse-drawn *bendis*, oxcarts loaded with various things, bicycle traffic, women going to market with produce balanced in baskets on their heads, and people fetching water in long, hollow bamboo poles.

Harold wrote a form letter to all his supporters telling about this new place and their house.

"I remember when the Evangel was anchored in one of the rivers in Borneo, waiting to go. Our automobile was on the back deck and reached from one side to the other. One day Jerry Lanphear and I were playing on the back deck, and I tried to edge around the car but fell into the water. I can still vividly recall falling into the muddy brown water, seeing brown bubbles reach the surface, and thinking, 'There are crocodiles in this river!' Jerry let down a bucket (to pull me up?), but I swam to the back of the boat, where there was a ladder to climb up!" —Patsy

Tomohon, Minahasa, Sulawesi, Indonesia
June 1951
Our Dear Friends of Home,

We greet you from a new island in Indonesia this time, which may come as a surprise to many of you. For some time there has been a need for missionaries stationed on this island; and since returning this time, after much prayer and consideration, we felt God would have us make this move. The Evangel, our Speed the Light ship for the islands, brought us and the Lanphear family, who are working with us, to our new field.

Our trip from Bandjarmasin was a pleasant one, and after four and a half days of travel, we reached the harbor of Manado in Sulawesi (or Celebes, as it was formerly known) at 2:00 a.m. with everybody out on deck to catch the first dim view of Manado Tua, meaning Old Manado, a conical shaped mountain rising out of the sea. The coastline had been mountainous for quite a stretch before reaching the city of Manado, and we wondered as we sailed along the previous days, how many villages there were back in those mountains which had never heard the glorious message we had come to tell. Time will show us the opportunities there are back in these inland regions.

In the morning there was much to do to prepare to unload baggage and the car from the ship, since we were anchored out in the harbor. The children were left on the ship while we parents went on ahead to our new homes some 15 miles up in the mountains. The ladies received quite a surprise when they saw the new homes—new to us, but ready to fall apart otherwise. Most of the homes in Tomohon have never had paint, and all of them are very old. It seemed the best thing that could be obtained; and after all, it makes little difference what we live in, but the big thing is how we live and what we live for. We are living for God and desire to be used of Him in whatever phase of missionary work He should lead. We men had warned our womenfolk that the houses were not so nice, but perhaps it could not be visualized that they were quite as bad as they were. However, they took it well and only looked at one another and laughed. Now we are all used to it and realize that it is not the kind of house we live in that makes a home.

To describe the houses briefly, we might say they are mostly built up high on stilts, some even having a room built underneath with an earth floor. The wall boards, which run vertically, are of various sizes and colors of wood, with beams running across at most any angle and any place. The floors are so worm-eaten and old that they give as you walk across them, shaking the dishes or flower vases on the tables or in the cupboards. Brother Lanphear climbed up into the attic to make some electrical repairs, and suddenly the rest of the house heard a crashing sound and looked up to see his feet coming right through the ceiling. He did not fall through to the floor, but was bruised some. This shows how weak the old boards are. There are patches all over the house on the walls or doors or floors where rotted worm-eaten wood has been cut out in various sizes and shapes with newer pieces put in their place. One of our walls has four new boards put in, yet they are not new either, for they are worm-eaten too, but not as badly as the ones taken out. Our house once had a coat of paint (back in the days of Noah, perhaps) and we feel it would look better to have not had it, for all the repairs are unpainted. We have something in this house that we didn't have in Bandjarmasin, and that is glass in some of our windows, for it is very cool up here in the mountains, so much so that we must use a blanket at night. We use sweaters in the early mornings and late evenings, something we couldn't imagine doing in Indonesia. Our front room is all windows across the front and side, which open like doors; and can all be opened, allowing plenty of fresh air when desired. Thus, since the house is built high against a hill, we have a good view of the surrounding country and all that goes on.

We couldn't ask for the countryside to be more beautiful. We can see the "fire mountain," as it is called, a volcanic peak nearby. Everything grows in abundance, so we have more flowers, shrubbery, and trees than we have had in all our stay in Indonesia.

We know that you will not fail to pray for us in this new field of endeavor for the Lord, for we feel that God wants to do a great work here. We hope to have a Bible school for training native workers and really get to work, so the task is large, and we need His help and yours. God bless you for your letters, prayers, and offerings. We do appreciate it all more than we can tell you.

Most sincerely, your missionaries,

Harold & Jean Carlblom

Jean also filled in her parents on the new situation, and true to her optimistic nature, she tried to find the positive things.

Dearest Mother, Dad, Grandma, and Barbara,

We are located about 15 miles away from Manado. We are in the mountains, and we can see a volcano from the house. There is only one street until the center of town, and then it widens a street or two. But up in back of our house it rises up quite abruptly so it is difficult to climb, but it is beautiful and enticing. There is such a beautiful tropical growth here, vines and ferns galore and wild flowers; the kiddies have the time of their lives picking flowers morning and afternoon every day. They have never seen so many flowers anywhere, I guess. It is cool in the mornings until 9 or 10 and then it really warms up unless it is a rainy day. But if not, it is warm until about 4 or 5 and then it gets cool. We left all our blankets home, but Bro. Devin had quilts from W.M.C. [Women's Missionary Council] for missionaries so he gave us one for every bed for both families. So we keep warm at night.

It is damp a great deal, and the ground stays damp. We have quite a yard, but our house is high on stilts so it is dry; but it is very difficult to dry our clothes, and the sheets at night feel damp. The house is ground level in the back but high enough up in the front to have a basement room below the front (and stilts), then in back of that it is just empty space. We have a perfect setting for a rock garden at the side; in fact, a natural rock garden both sides, with rocks and wildflowers already growing. There is a little channel cut for water to run through when it rains so it runs in a stream on both sides of the house off the yard. And this runs through this sort of rock garden which we want to work on and fix nice. Another disadvantage is the house. I never saw such houses in all my life. Of course, there are so very few Europeans here that all houses are native built. This is old as the hills, but has had paint on it in the past. But there are beams running every which way in the house. Some windows don't even have frames around them, no sills, all the wood is worm-eaten. Really the house would have long ago been condemned had it been in America. Then it is so old. The beams around the front room are so worm-eaten they look like sponge. I don't think I could describe it to you so you could really see it. You couldn't imagine it at home. The floors are wide boards like in Borneo but so weak, so worm-eaten that, as the kiddies run across the floor, everything shakes and the windows rattle. Yes, we have glass in our windows, and I mean lots of it. The whole front of the front room is glassed; the windows open swinging out, and you bring the two sides in and fasten in the middle together. Each window has 12 panes of glass in it, and there are 3 big windows across the front, each half having 12 panes making lots of panes in our front and dining rooms. The bedrooms don't have so many. I cleaned the front windows today. We close the house up around 7 to keep warm, though tonight is warmer, and I am comfortable. But if we go to Manado it is very hot there, just like Bandjar. There is a wide stairway on either side of the house leading you up to the door, then a narrow porch bringing you back toward the front of the house so you enter into the front room, which is L-shaped, making a front and dining room and still some other kind of room. It is quite roomy. So for once we have all kinds of room. There are 3 bedrooms, so Jo has her own. The children's rooms have cement floors so they can run all they want, but all through the rest of the house it surely shakes. The paint is so old and several different colors and shades. And many of the panes of glass are broken so we always have fresh air, though some have been boarded up so much that one bedroom door is all wood panels instead of the glass panes, which is just as well. They painted over some glass that remained, and it gives a different shade. And the paint is so old. We would like to paint but have to do it ourselves and pay for it also ourselves. There is so much repairing to be done, but we just can't afford it. But paint might cover up the rotten beams. There is no molding around the floors, and the boards are rotten and worm-eaten at the ends terribly so you can sweep and sweep and sweep some more and never get it clean. Our cupboards all lean to one side or the front or back because the floors are so uneven. When we washed the floors, the water all ran out of the bedrooms into the dining room. It is so dirty and dusty and the kind that just does not come clean. But we are brushing and scrubbing away. I couldn't dust the window ledges around the glass because a duster gets all stuck in the rough wood, but I used a broom because I had no brush and the broom was as good as nothing, finally used my fingers and nails. When it was painted formerly they got lots of paint on the glass around the edges too and that doesn't help the appearance any. But we are missionaries, so we just got to work and cleaned it up best we could. Wish I could paint the bedroom to go with the bedspread and drapes, but if we paint it'll only be the front room.

I want to tell you about the kitchen and back part of the house. The back part of the house is separate, but a walk joins one to the other. It is to the side and off from the back door. It is like one room after another going up the hill. First is the "mandi" (bathroom or shower room). Then you go up the stairs and to the toilet. They call that the "little room." The floors of these rooms are cement and so poor and broken that one is just like a bunch of big stones side by side. The kitchen is all broken up, too, and then has a big cement-frame tabletop filled in with dirt to make a flat surface for your fires—just made like a bonfire around rocks. It is very crude. They don't even burn charcoal, but coconut shells and some wood (though that is high in price). We have to walk several blocks for our drinking water, though we have "baks" [big cement tanks] to catch rainwater right here, though not large. Water is a problem. Where we get our water, it looks like a fish pond, and they say the water comes from a spring, but to make it accessible for everyone, they pipe it from one pond to another, piped with bamboo, and this runs back of the houses across the street all the way down. Each family gets water from their own pond. But it looks milky, and though you can see it is constantly running, there are pond plants that grow on it. At the place ours comes out is a place for people to bathe, too. But what we don't like is that it is downhill in back of all these houses. Is that clean? So we started boiling rainwater.

In our toilet there is a big cement block with a hollow in it on which you stand and squat—different style, huh? Barb, I sure wish you could see the house. I can just hear you scream and say, "No—I'm dreaming, is it really like this, Jean?"

"I can remember more than once being scared out of the outhouse because of a rat going down the hole."
—Patsy

And when you see our big spiders here and hear the wild animals howl at night, and the place is full of rats and mice. And—we went to the market yesterday, which is more primitive than Borneo, we saw them selling baked rats. That is quite the thing here.

The Lord has been very real to us and has blessed us in prayer. We feel He has a work for us here, though we don't know yet exactly what that will be. Leonard is supposed to be in charge of the Bible school when we get one started, though we will all help. Harold is in charge of evangelizing and also is sort of a presbyter or something over the island. The object is to visit around and help in these churches that are interested in joining the Assemblies. We are not expected to open a church ourselves, but if we find a capable man in the section, we can use him and help him start something here later on. We could start out holding services or Sunday school in these rooms below. We are looking for God to lead, but feel something will open up and all things work out for His glory.

Today the men put in some American plug-ins so we can use our toaster and electric iron. We have been eating out until yesterday when we got settled.

Now I think I will stop, but more will come. We'll let you know what we are doing and more about the country. Very hard to buy anything here for yourself, for the house, or to eat—stuff we eat, anyhow. Have no cook yet. Bye for now.

We love you lots,

Jean and Harold

The hill also was a great vantage point to view the volcano, which was about eight kilometers away. It had periodic eruptions. The Carlbloms would be alerted to it by an earthquake and then would run up there to watch the clouds of volcanic ash belch out of the crater. Sometimes if the wind was coming their way, an ashfall would come later, and everything would be covered by fine ash.

When they lived in Minahasa, Patsy made a lifelong friend. Loesje Rooroh lived fairly close by, and the

"I can remember loving to go up on the hill behind our house and into the woods. I would bring paper or a notebook and write stories, as I had the desire to be an author when I grew up."

—Patsy

Loesje Rooroh and Patsy. *Charlaine with Loesje.*

two girls would sometimes leave notes for each other in the *jambu* (guava) tree. Patsy invited her to church, and she became a Christian and eventually influenced her whole family. In fact, several of the extended family even entered the ministry.

> *Dear Mother, Dad, Grandma and Barb,*
>
> *Mother, you asked just where we are. You know Indonesia is made up of many, many islands, five of which are a good size. These main ones are Borneo [now Kalimantan], New Guinea, Java, Sumatra, and Celebes [now Sulawesi]. We are in Sulawesi, a long, narrow island to the east of Borneo, and it rises farther north, too. We are in the upper tip where it curls around. Manado is a seacoast town, and one of the largest towns. Sulawesi is the name of our island, Tomohon is the village we live in, and Minahasa is not a state but*

an area, this northern tip. Now you have it all straight. Our mail comes up here now, and we call for it at the post office. By the way—speaking of an office, I want to tell you about one which is typical of all. I went in this office to attend to some business while Harold was away. There were tables all through the room, and because they have no built-ins, they were piled high with papers and letters and things—in neat piles. Each pile had a huge stone on it, which they use for paperweights. They have to have them on everything, because the houses and offices are so open, and if a breeze comes, or if they use a fan, everything blows all over. But it looks so strange to see every table with three or four piles of neatly stacked papers with stones on them.

There are no "becas" here (those were the bicycle carts). But here we have the "bendis"—those are pony carts. There were none of those in Borneo. You would enjoy a ride in a bendi. As you step in, the cart gives a little and is sort of wobbly until you get settled. One time a couple of weeks ago we got in one, and the horse was tired. It was evening, and he was a very skinny horse and had a busy day, I guess, and he refused to go. The man whipped and whipped him—we felt sorry for the horse and tried to get out, but the guy didn't want to lose the business and was insisting the pony go. The pony even bucked, and that is bad, because they can tip, and they may go into the ditch. We were quite uneasy, and finally got out when he quit kicking around. The next one did better and trotted right off, and we went bouncing on our way. The girls love it. But of course we have the car, and there is no place to go in a town like this, so we seldom ride one. We are getting used to hearing the "trot-trot" of horses down the street now. I remember when I was a little girl and we used to go to see you, [Grandma], and you lived upstairs somewhere near downtown, I thought, and we used to hear horses go by. Am I dreaming, or is it so? Anyway, when I hear that "trot-trot," I am taken back to those days, looking out of an upstairs window and hearing the horses—maybe a milkman or something— I don't know.

I have a sweater on now, but the kiddies seem happy without one. It is 4:00 o'clock. We can eat soup here and enjoy it. In fact, it is cooler here than we like. We got used to the heat, and though this is a relief, we want it "just right," you know. Stone or tile floors would be cold, so we are satisfied with our old wooden floors. Guess it doesn't matter what you live in, that isn't what makes happiness, is it? But if you sit down and look at our surroundings in the house, it would be nice to look at a polished floor instead of old bumpy, uneven, dusty-looking boards, no paint "no nothing" on them. And I would like my wall either painted or not. Part is—part isn't. And half my window sills are eaten off—they have cancer, I guess. We do have lots of flowers in the house, though, and I use every vase I've got, and bowls too. We have our portable organ up in the front room, and our chair set, which consists of 4 rattan chairs and table, and today we bought a small bamboo table and two chairs to match. I have two other small tables here and there, and still there is lots of room. The room is large. We have no furniture for Joanne's room yet, but must order it to be made. That is kind of bad, because you never know what they will make in the end. But she has to have something, and we haven't been able to buy anything suitable on a "lelang" [auction] yet. They have several a week, and everyone goes to them just to have something to do, if nothing else.

We haven't gotten started in the work or meetings yet much but will write about that later.

> "I can remember eating a spicy snack with my sisters, and Marjorie would have tears running down her cheeks from the heat of the peppers, but she would still want more!"
> —Patsy

While the house may not have been something out of a magazine, it was always filled with love. Both Jean and Harold showed their affection for each other and for their daughters very freely. Harold nicknamed them "dolly" or "honeybunch" or "sweetie-pie," and all the girls remember seeing Jean and Harold share long kisses, which never embarrassed the children, but seemed very natural. Their parents' love for each other was always evident, and their love for their daughters was unquestioned. Harold would often compose a poem for special occasions through the years, in which his love for his family was expressed.

Truly, whether at home in the States or on the other side of the world, The Carlbloms were themselves. Sometimes it was the couple sharing a kiss. Other times, it was Jean and her endless curiosity. After all, many aspects of missionary life was so intriguing, especially to her. She was always interested in people's stories, and she had a knack for drawing them out. She went on bike rides with Patsy, and she often took a new path to "see what might be down there." In one letter home, she wrote: "Things get to be common, but I never cease to wonder about things. We pass these little bamboo shacks, and I have a real urge to go inside this one or that and find out all about those people and how they live and what they do. We do know about their lives to a certain extent, but I guess you never really know them until you live with them."

Along with a different house, and new places to explore, this move came with a change in food options. Indonesia has many regional cuisines, and the specialties of the Minahasa area became the favorites of the family. Known as *Manadonese* cuisine, it was known for the generous use of various spices. At noon they typically ate the large meal of the day, which consisted of various meats, fish, or vegetables in a sauce served over rice, the primary staple. Indonesian food has influences of Chinese and Indian cuisines, and in the Minahasa area, it was usually quite spicy from hot peppers.

Adjustments came in many areas of life—even when it came to pets. The Carlblom family had the usual cats and dogs as pets in Tomohon, but also monkeys and a cockatoo. The first monkey became sick, and the girls kept him in a doll cradle and fed him with a dropper, but sadly, he died. Later a new monkey—a small black one—got used to being carried around like a baby doll, particularly by Charlaine. In addition, the family dog gave birth to puppies, so the task soon became finding homes for them. The Minahasan people were known for eating dogs, so the Carlbloms did their best to keep a close eye on their pets—and to give the puppies to people who wanted pets, not food.

"We had the usual dogs and cats, but we also had exotic, colorful, tropical parrots and a majestic white cockatoo. My favorites were the monkeys. We almost always had a monkey or two. They were so much fun because they were so humanlike. They were very affectionate and would cling, hugging me as they did their mothers in the jungle. I used to dress them up in doll clothes and take them for rides in my doll buggy. Sometimes I fed them in my doll highchair. It was like having a live doll!"
—Charlaine

The Carlbloms and the Lanphears soon began holding evangelistic services to start a nucleus of believers in the areas surrounding Tomohon. Another form letter to supporting churches went out from Harold in July 1951.

Our Dear Friends of Home,

We welcome the opportunity of penning a few lines to you, for it refreshes our memories of you all and the happy associations we had during our furlough. It is our sincere hope that this letter will serve as another pleasant visit.

Perhaps our visit will be more enjoyable if you accompany us to a mountain village service. The road is rough and poor and crowded with many ox and pony carts, bicycles, and foot pedestrians—so we travel slowly, seeing house after house of bamboo with "atap" roofs [palm leaves sewed together]. Since the main occupation is the raising of coconuts, these palms are everywhere. Coffee bushes, clove trees, and other spice and fruit trees are in abundance, with flowers galore. When we come to the house where the meeting will be held, we are met by many people, for they have heard that we are coming. As we sit on the porch visiting, waiting till the time for service, we are served warm, weak tea with cakes made of rice flour and coconut; or it may be rice rolled and cooked in banana leaves. Many folks stand on the porch or gaze from neighboring windows as we eat.

Charlaine with pet monkey.

The first nights the meeting was held in the house and porch, but moved out into the yard under an atap [thatched] shelter as the crowds increased nightly. We rarely have seen such interest as we watched their faces during the messages, just drinking in every word. Most of the people are standing, and among them many children, but there is still not a bit of disturbance, except for the coughing and choking of one child after another, for whooping cough is going through the town. It thrills our hearts as we see them crowded so close around where we sit and play our instruments. They are on both sides and front and back of us, some on the porches or wherever they could manage. We cannot estimate the number, for they are so many. Many hands are raised for prayer, and only eternity will reveal what has been done. They begged us to come back again and "please bring the children." The little ones had stayed at home to make room for others who wanted to come.

After the service is over, they insist that we stay and eat; and since it is all planned and prepared, we cannot refuse, although the hour is late. As we sit at the table with the preacher and some of the men, the women are busy watching our every need, bringing us new dishes of delicious food to put on our rice, urging us to eat more. The amusing thing, though, is the crowd of children and grownups right behind our chairs, or those gazing in through the windows and doors—even from neighboring houses we see them piling one on top of another to watch us. We never have eaten before such an audience, so we have to guard our facial expressions if there is something we don't like.

Though we're pushing our way to the car, the crowd still doesn't move until the car starts rolling, and then "goodbye" and "come again" are called out as they stretch out their hands to catch ours as we pass. It is a welcome that inspires and draws us back, and we feel that God wants to do a special work in this area. Will you pray with us that His Spirit will be outpoured in an unusual way and His power manifest in the saving of many souls with signs and wonders following? We feel that God wants to do something special if we are faithful, do our part and let Him take control. Pray much for us and this work.

Your faithful servant in Christ,

Harold Carlblom

Eating a meal after the services seemed as strange to the Carlbloms as it was for the villagers. The people crowded the doors and windows, watching them eat. It was apparently a novelty to see white people—and to watch them eat! Sometimes the missionaries didn't know just what they were eating, as the meat could be in a sauce or mixed in with vegetables. However, Minahasan people were known for eating dog meat—and also bat and rat meat. In fact, the missionaries were told by many people that even though they never *knowingly* ate those meats, since they lived in Minahasa as long as they did, they surely did eat them!

This unusual dietary issue, while unappetizing to American tastes (to say the least), was not the greatest hardship. Bad news arrived around this time and is explained in this excerpt of an undated letter:

> *We just received the tragic news of Brother Ralph Devin's death. It has come as such a shock to all of us. We can hardly believe it, for we were all together on the ship not so long ago, and we did get well acquainted with him on those trips. We saw in him so many wonderful qualities as a leader for us here, and he had such a good understanding of everything, and such a vision of the work. We can't see that anyone can take his place, but only God knows. His ways are best, and we cannot question. We shall miss him greatly, not only as a leader here, but as a friend. He was always so understanding, so sweet in spirit and so kind.*
>
> *He was a man who was always the same, in the hardest moments, no matter what criticism was flung at him, no matter in what spirit hard things were said to him; he was calm, didn't raise his voice, never showed anger, and had a smile. He wouldn't hurt anyone. Being this sort, he kept all his feelings in, and it was hard on him and his nerves, evidently, and he had no strength to fight the malaria.*

Another difficulty living in a foreign country was dealing with customs, which wasn't an issue only when arriving in country. Packages coming from the States were often opened, and sometimes the contents were pilfered along the way.

Dear Mother & Dad & Grandma & Barbara,

We got a package yesterday, sent April tenth, all baby bottles for Urens, but nothing else in it. It was a wreck when it came—had been opened by customs, in how many places we don't know. Harold said he was in the post office in Manado the other day, and they had packages opened for customs and just strewn all over. Then I suppose they take out what they want. Anyhow, the declaration slip said notepaper and magazines, and was dated March something, so the wrong slip was on the wrong package, which makes it look like they came through customs together, but one was taken. But why would anyone take paper and magazines? What magazines were they? Perhaps Pat's Children's Activities? Was that reordered for her? She is starved for something to read, and is reading everything all over. This makes her dig into the Book of Knowledge, too, for other things besides stories. Now she is reading biographies and Book of Wonder. She reads Jo's American Literature, too. We don't have the book of Huck Finn, which you could buy with our funds and enclose in a package. Then we can give it to her for a birthday or Christmas or something.

*P.S. Charlaine (three years old) announced, "Margie is getting to be a big girl, and **I** am a grown-up."*

Love, Jean and Harold

The Carlbloms began holding services in the ground-level room under their house. Also, many people had needs, so a lot of counseling and visiting with them kept Harold busy. They also launched plans to build simple buildings for the Minahasa Bible School, which would be located near the Lanphears' house in Kakaskasen, an area of Tomohon.

While their parents worked for the mission, the children often played an Indonesian game something like

Deetje (Marj's friend), Marj, Charlaine, and Jeanne (Deetje's sister).

softball, but with only two bases and a softer ball. Their large front yard was the perfect gathering place for games with neighborhood kids. A rubber tree in the yard provided hours of play. They could make rubber balls by cutting a slash in the tree, spreading the sap on a banana leaf, and letting it dry. Then they would roll the dried sap into a ball, and presto—their own (bumpy) balls!

While the girls made the transition to new surroundings, Jean continued writing letters to keep in contact with her family back in the States. Her newsy letters always contained much about the household and their friends—and often reports of their mission work and her own spiritual journey.

> *Dear Mother,*   *1951*
>
> *I have felt a nearness of the Lord in prayer that I never had before. I enjoy prayer much more than I ever had*

and feel the presence of the Lord as I never have. I feel the Lord wants us to give ourselves more to prayer, and perhaps a deeper consecration. We do so want to see Him work and don't want anything hindering. Our time may be short, and there are so many outside the fold. We have always been so busy doing, doing; and I feel for my part, I have neglected prayer, not only for lack of time, but perhaps because I didn't get the satisfaction out of it I should have. But what does all the doing accomplish? We missionaries discussed this on the ship (Evangel); and it seemed that if we would all give ourselves to prayer, even though we didn't do anything else, we would be bound to see a move for God. We are not satisfied with the crowds and the interest, but we want souls, we want to see the unusual. Our hearts are crying out for something different, and we must be willing to pay the price in prayer. Pray much with us that God will work in and through us, that He will have His way in molding our lives, so that we can be used of Him.

We hear from Bandjarmasin that God is moving; two more have received the baptism and another the gift of prophecy. Hartimedes was praying about his needs, which were pressing, materially, and God was wonderfully close to him. He was enclosed by a wonderful light, saw it come down and encircle him, and then he heard the Voice telling him to trust and He would supply all his needs. He was so encouraged.

Dad said he had sent two packages, one in March and one in April, one containing four films, and another with books or magazines for Patsy, (that child, she reads everything there is to read—even reads Joanne's American Literature now—poems or stories, it doesn't matter) but you said in your June fourth letter that only one had been sent, containing baby bottles for Mrs. Uren. Urens lost their baby—I'm sure I told you? Just before we left, almost all the new babies in the hospital at that time died from something—they don't know what. One lady took her baby home early and it lived, but Urens' baby got fever the second day, was given an injection, and died that night. Four other babies died that day—no rash or anything, just a fever, but it must have been something contagious, which they will never know. He was a nice, healthy, fat boy, very sweet. She is staying in Banjar now because it is too dangerous inland and she is afraid to stay alone. He is gone three times a week, and overnight one or two of those nights. She has the children with her, of course.

Along with the work of starting a Bible school and sharing the gospel, the missionary families worked to create relationships with people in the area. Harold and Leonard Lanphear were invited to attend the funeral of a *Hukum Tua* (village elder) who was the head of a village nearby. Harold described their experience in a letter:

We drove over this very rocky road until we came to the village, and there we saw a sight that made us feel like turning back. There were seven men dressed in peculiar-looking garb, each of them with swords or native-type knives and shields. Their clothes were all red, and there were a lot of long, red, ragged tassels hanging all around them. They had wrapped yards of material around their middles so they looked fat, and their red trousers were short so that their muscular legs were very obvious as they went through their dancing. Six of them wore hats that were covered with feather plumes, and the seventh (the leader) wore a large brass helmet of the ancient warrior type. One of them carried a native drum, and as he started beating it, they all took on a devilish look and sort of crouched position, and began a snaky-looking dance, all the time brandishing their weapons and charging toward the house (they were outside, as were most of the people) and then retreating and charging again and again. Finally they got to the house and then, since it was crowded and small, they filed in to the casket (a wooden box covered with black cloth. Here also, they went through some chanting and dancing before the casket. After they came out, the casket was brought outside, and once again they repeated much of the former, charging the casket and waving their swords and shouting and singing. It was a weird sight, to say the least. This sort of ceremony is carried on only in the case of headmen who have died.

Experiences like this made it clear to the missionaries that much work lay ahead. Even so, they were encouraged by invitations from people who had become Christians through some of the other mission works in the country who would invite the Carlbloms and Lanphears to visit and hold services. Initially these meetings were held in their homes, sometimes with a lean-to built alongside. The missionaries brought instruments, and the music would draw in people who were curious—there's not a lot going on in these small villages—and then a salvation message would be preached. Many people responded to the call, and that would form the nucleus of a new church. However, until the Bible school began producing graduates, there would not be leaders for these new congregations. For the intervening time, the missionaries needed to visit these fledgling churches regularly.

The Lanphears and Carlbloms often held services in a town called Langoan, about 20 miles away from Tomohon. In that area military posts existed in a few places because of the unrest and trouble. When passing these posts, if there was a guard, the missionaries needed to stop and show their papers, which had to be carried at all times. Sometimes even then the guards would be suspicious and search through all the instrument cases. At times they even looked under the automobile seats to see if the missionaries were carrying any arms.

One night they passed through a village where they were stopped, and when the guards realized they were ministers driving to a meeting, they simply waved the car on. Along the road, beyond the village but not too far out in the country—where there were no houses—they were stopped again by a pair of men. These two weren't in uniform, but they approached the car, one each side. One man brandished a knife—a terrible, big, long knife—and the other held a pistol. Stopping the car, the men asked, rather hesitantly, where they were from and where they were going, as usual, and then let them go. The Carlbloms and Lanphears learned later that guards were stationed only right in the villages, and then always in uniform. Some told the missionaries it must have been because the apparent bandits saw three men in the front seat that they let them go. Perhaps one of their prayer partners back in the U.S. was prompted to pray at that moment. Truly, God's protection was covering them.

Meeting in the villages didn't always seem dangerous, but often it wasn't easy. No large buildings existed in these rural settlements, so they had to make do. From time to time, the Carlbloms bought some *atap* (palm leaves) sewed together for a roof to use in Langoan and elsewhere for their meetings, for homes were too small. The roof was put off to the side of some house so the house served as one wall, and the other wall was made of boards in the rough, or sometimes just strips of palm leaves hanging down all around. The ground was the floor and served the purpose unless it rained. The folks would just kneel right on the ground.

Erecting a shelter for a meeting place was one thing, but dealing with erupting volcanoes was quite another, as they described in a letter:

Twice lately, in one day, six hours apart, the mountain erupted; and did it ever shake the house that time! And the dust or "abu" [ashes] came this way. Usually the wind carries most of it farther away, but that day it came right here, so it was hard to breathe, and it covered all our rainwater. Lanphears are a kilometer closer to the mountain, and they got it an inch thick all around their house.

Did we tell you in our last letter about some meetings we were holding the other side of Manado? We went every day at about 5:00 or 5:30. We had to go down the mountain and through Manado on to this place. On the way we crossed a stream quite deep down, but of course went over a bridge, an old fashioned wooden covered bridge. One night, coming home we passed it about 10:00 p.m. At 10:15 some guerillas making trouble burned the bridge. We didn't know about it until we were ready to leave the next day and got a telephone call that the bridge had burned from a truck. We thought it rather strange that a truck should burn while on the bridge, and wondered why they didn't go to the other side and get out and let the truck burn, and finally we concluded that it must have exploded. That night we had to go another way. There is only one other way to go—about the same distance, but not such a good road, and more curves. On the way, we were stopped by a string of cars lined up on the road, and when we looked ahead we saw a tree had been cut down on a cliff above the road and had fallen the wrong way. We sat there for almost an hour, waiting for men to saw through it and roll part of it off so cars could go through. We asked about the bridge being burned the other way and were told by some men in a military truck that guerillas had burned it and that it was dangerous even on this road now.

We thought then that it might be better to go right back, but folks were expecting us for a meal and service. We were already late, or would be an hour late, so thought we'd better go on. On the way we had crossed another bridge on this road identical to the one the other way that had been burned.

The night we saw the tree across the road, the kids were along. While waiting, the kids went in some caves right there where we were parked to wait. There are two places up in the mountains where there are a number of big caves, large enough for trucks to go through. Inside there are a number of passageways going all directions. They have been wired with electricity, too. They were built by forced labor during the war, the Japanese forcing the Indonesians. The Japanese used them for their military camps, for their troops, supplies, and for safety from bombs. Often we had passed some ten or more caves on another road, and the kiddies had longed to explore them, so now was their chance to explore these while waiting. Bats had their homes there, and of course they flew all around their heads, reminding them of Tom Sawyer and Becky, lost in a cave, and the bats putting out their candles by flying against them; but they had a flashlight, so the bats did them no harm. That night after we had come home, that covered bridge was also burned by the guerillas. We felt the Lord had definitely been with us.

"I still have memories of those trips to surrounding towns. I remember one area where there were caves along the side of the road that had been used during the Japanese occupation of the war. We stopped to look at them, but I thought they were spooky and had bats in them, so I didn't want to venture inside."

—Patsy

Our girls are living in a realm of excitement with all this. They like all the excitement. When this second bridge was burned, it was the last night of our meetings there, so we were not hindered in our meetings. Charlaine and Marjorie hear the local kids talking, and the version they get from the stories is really something. Charlaine is awfully scared, though, more so than Marj, and always talking about a "jahat" [wicked] man. She runs screaming if she sees a man pass by with a knife.

We had another "tjelaka" today. A tjelaka is an accident or mishap. On Wednesday, the first day of the

> *conference, the cook used the meat grinder. Today we thought our meatballs tasted funny but ate them anyway. After dinner the cook told me she couldn't get the meat grinder loose from the table or open, either, to wash it. On questioning, I found that it hasn't been washed for six days and was used again today—no wonder the meat tasted rotten. On opening it, we found the meat in it was black and full of worms. I feel a pain right now!! Grandma would probably faint on the spot. I couldn't look at those white maggots in it. She did say she wiped it off inside with the dishcloth the best she could, but the dishcloth is far from clean, especially the way they take care of it here, black as all get-out, and slimy. I had just been instructing her about it, because when I used it I found it so slimy and dirty, so I told her to wash it daily. That was a must, but here she used it on the grinder. Guess I'd better not mail this until I see how we all come out on this so you won't worry. We could all get food poisoning. Pat, Marj, and Charlaine didn't eat any. We had company, the C.M.A. [Christian and Missionary Alliance] preacher, so we knelt down and asked God's protection on our bodies. (Written in later: We're okay—this is the next day. So don't worry, Grandma.)*
>
> *Jean and Harold*

Of course they expected the occasional *tjelaka*, but another one of the hard things they faced as missionaries was being separated from extended family. Harold wrote:

> *We think of you all so often and wonder why it is we can't be with you all, and enjoy your presence as other people can, but this is the BIG SACRIFICE that we feel as missionaries. It is not the discomforts or lack of opportunity to get the things we could in America. Those are trivial things! But we do feel the long time between our chances of seeing all of you, our dear, dear loved ones! However, I'm sure the Lord has been very*

good to us and has and is making it all up, so we won't be the losers.

Jean voiced some of those same feelings in a letter of hers:

We enjoy your letters as they come—and all the news—so much. We look forward so to your letters—you don't know how much, I'm sure. I guess you look for ours, too, but then you have some of your own near, which satisfies to a certain extent, and we have no one of the family, and a letter means so very much.

The Carlbloms weren't the only ones dealing with difficulties. Poor Mary Jane Lanphear struggled with extreme weakness and pain so much of the time. In reading of her symptoms, it sounds much like what is described now in fibromyalgia; but at that time, no such thing was diagnosed. She took iron shots and multivitamins, but to no avail. The concern about her health was so serious that it was decided at the missionary conference that the Lanphears should return to the States early for their furlough.

The Lanphears were scheduled to leave Indonesia in August of 1952, and it was decided that Joanne would return with them and stay with Jean's parents as she finished high school. Jean and Harold struggled with the decision, as Joanne was only 16 and they would not be seeing her for two and a half years, but it seemed the best decision because she wanted to finish high school in the States. Besides, no other missionaries would be heading home before the Carlbloms, so it was her only opportunity to travel with companions. It was a double loss for Jean, as she was losing both her daughter and a close friend.

Even so, Jean was used to sacrifice, and her many responsibilities would continue to keep her busy. Jean wrote about her schedule in September of 1952:

Dear family at home,

We have been very busy. I helped in the Bible school too, and when Morris Devin came, I was relieved somewhat but still teach a class a day. It has helped me in the language, and I have sort of enjoyed it too. But it keeps me awfully busy—no time to sew or anything extra. Get up, pray, breakfast, family prayer, start school with the girls by 8:00 or 8:30. It takes about two hours for Marj, and I have to sit right there. Then when she finishes, I help Pat until noon. After dinner from 1:00 on I take time to read and pray and then study for school; and then whatever time I am not in class, I arrange Patsy's papers and correct arithmetic and try to write a letter or fix flannelgraphs or clean cupboards or bake, but time just flies, and suddenly it is 6:00. It takes time to go to and from school, so my class time is about an hour, and once a week I speak in chapel. Then we eat and rush off to service six nights a week, and get home 10, 11, or 11:30, depending on where we are going. So you see where the time goes.

We had some shooting about 3:30 in the morning last week and it happened three times, machine guns one time, and the other two just a single shot. The next day we got news that police were patrolling and were fired on with one killed and three wounded. It was guerillas. They are not too far from here, but it is seldom that anything happens so close. But there was a little row a month or so ago in a place we go for meetings, and it happened on a night we were supposed to go and couldn't. Several were killed there. That was the military and police, because the police are in control now, not the military. There are still guerillas, but not much actual trouble.

Thankfully, the unrest stayed mostly away from the Carlbloms, and Harold's days were as full as Jean's. Harold's schedule in the early days in Minahasa involved supervising some of the building of the dormitories and church in Tomohon. He also was preparing the curriculum for some of the Bible school classes, often interpreting them from English. Throughout his missionary career, prayer and Bible reading was an important part of his schedule. His children often heard him pray in his bedroom for hours at a time—sometimes alone, and sometimes with Jean. After the Bible school was operating, he taught several classes. Part of his time was also spent visiting and dealing with the many Indonesian leaders in the various churches. Studying for sermons was also a priority, as he had much to prepare for several services a week in the various churches throughout Minahasa.

The Bible school was up and underway with twelve students in the fall of 1952. Part of the delay had been the slow process of building dormitories for the students, as most of them came from a distance and needed a place to stay. The cost to run the Bible school had been underestimated, so they needed the students to work a certain number of hours in order to help out.

One thing that seemed to be difficult, both in the churches and in the Bible school, was for the nationals to be ready to contribute. They looked to the Americans as sources of unending funds, and the missionaries tried to instill in them the responsibility of giving themselves but sometimes gave out of their personal funds to help.

As busy as the schedule was, special occasions were sprinkled here and there. In 1953 Morris Devin, the son of Edna and Ralph Devin (pioneer missionaries to Indonesia) got married. The February wedding was a time of great excitement for all of the missionaries and their children. Morris's fiancée, Joyce Munger, came out from the U.S., and even the girls participated in the wedding and had special long dresses made for the occasion.

In April the Carlblom family took an overdue vacation, going to Ambon, Bali, and Java. And yet it really wasn't a vacation—they held services in Ambon and Java, and Jean kept the kids going in their schooling. She also tried to catch up on her correspondence with the many churches that helped support them. In one of her letters home, she said she had to write 19 letters a day to catch up! Jean's typewriter always got a workout!

The Carlbloms did have some fun on their vacation. They stayed for a few days in Selecta, a resort in the mountains above Surabaya, Java. It was a lovely place with beautiful surroundings, and an ice-cold swimming pool with a tall water slide. The girls went on the slide numerous times and even talked Jean into joining them.

"I remember the wild roses growing beside the path we walked to get to the swimming pool, and I remember eating strawberries while we were there, a rarity in Indonesia!" —Patsy

Back in Tomohon again, life resumed at its busy pace, with services several times a week, Bible school classes to teach, as well as Sunday school classes. For teaching classes, the curriculum was all adapted and interpreted from English material, and Jean would try to find flannelgraph figures to fit the stories. In addition, there was the girls' Calvert School studies to supervise. The work seemed never-ending. Harold's desk was stacked with books used for translating three of his classes and two of Jean's. At this time, Harold was teaching fifteen classes a week, but was relieved somewhat when the Lanphears returned from furlough. He still taught eight classes after that.

Jean also kept busy with piano lessons for both Marj and Patsy, as well as two of their friends from the church, Deetje and Patsy's best friend, Loesje. So there were four students doing their daily practicing, which sometimes drove Jean almost crazy, hearing the same songs over and over!

Marjorie and Deetje.

While the girls weren't busy with schoolwork or piano practice, they did typical things that all kids do—including getting into mischief. Marjorie remembers an episode involving a *lemari*.

A *lemari* was a common article of furniture in Indonesia. It was wardrobe or cabinet, typically made of wood and used for food, clothing, or other supplies, since there were never any built-in closets or cupboards. If the *lemari* held food, there would always be a tuna can filled with water under the legs, so as to keep the ants away from the food.

Music lessons, mischief, and tuna cans aside, they moved on once again to deal with other issues. Other challenges significantly worse. For example, the dry season in Minahasa runs from

"One day my sister Charlaine and I decided to climb some shelving in a lemari and sit on the top, because it sounded like fun! I climbed up first, and when Charlaine followed me and stepped on the second shelf, it broke—and two beautiful vases fell and broke into what seemed like a million pieces. The servant girl heard the crash and came running.

'You are in trouble!'

'Why am I in trouble? Charlaine's the one who broke the shelf!'

But something about responsibility as the older sister was invoked, and we both ended up with a spanking from our parents!"

—*Marjorie*

April to October, and although the Carlbloms had dug a well to help with the water supply, there were problems with that. A bad odor grew evident, and a dead rat was found in the well. Soon afterward they also discovered a dead mouse in the big cistern that caught the rainwater, so water had to be fetched from the spring across the street until the cistern was drained and cleaned and more rainwater was collected.

One continual concern was the unrest in the country. Guerillas still roamed, causing problems here and there. At one point a guerilla who had just been released from 26 months in jail came to visit and asked to borrow Harold's car—and a pistol! Harold told him he had no pistol but later said he didn't think the man believed him. He did not lend the car. After that incident, whenever Harold traveled to help in other areas, he arranged for a couple of the Bible school students to stay in the room beneath the house to provide security for Jean and the girls.

As 1954 began, the Carlbloms began to look toward furlough. In one letter to her parents, Jean wrote that, although they would really like to be back for Joanne's high school graduation, doing so would be cutting their term short to three and a half years instead of four.

Little time passed before a letter arrived from the Asia Field Secretary in the States, Rev. Howard Osgood. He explained that if it was okay with the missionary chairman of the field, they could return in time for the graduation! It seems that Joanne had taken it upon herself to write Brother Osgood to see if it might be possible. The Indonesia Field Chairman, Rev. John Tinsman, agreed, so Jean and Harold began plans for the trip in the spring of 1954, in time for Jo's graduation.

What a blessing it was to reunite as a family for this special occasion! During this furlough, they lived

"I had lots of friends at church, and eagerly looked forward to each weekend when we would have Hi C.A.'s (junior high service) and then the regular Christ Ambassador service for all teens. The year passed quickly—too quickly, for me, as I hated to leave all the friends I had made at church. It was about this time that I developed a crush on Bob Pearson, but he was shy around girls, and I was only fourteen, so it was a secret crush. I always thought of him when I heard the song 'Once I had a Secret Love.'" —Patsy

A photo of the Carlblom family wearing traditional Indonesian dress, as it appeared in the Minneapolis Star.

in a rented house on Fifteenth Avenue South in Minneapolis. It was good for Joanne to be back with the family again, and Patsy remembers times of sisterly fun—and advice on how to wear a scarf. Joanne had been dating Dick Balken, whose father pastored a church in Northeast Minneapolis; it was a time of obvious change for Harold and Jean—their girls were growing up. A year might seem like a long time when looking at the upcoming calendar, but time passed quickly with itineration meetings and time spent reconnecting with family in person. Suddenly, it seemed, the year was over.

Chapter 7

More Time in Sulawesi: Third Term

Then the nations will know that I am the LORD.
—Ezekiel 36:23

The Carlbloms went back to Indonesia for their third term in July of 1956, flying through Japan, Hong Kong, and Bangkok, and seeing other missionaries along the way.

When they got back to Indonesia, it was time for the Field Conference of the Assemblies of God in Indonesia, and Harold was elected Field Chairman. He was encouraged that some of the nationals who had graduated from the various Bible schools were beginning to take places of leadership. Even so, this transition was slow going, until it was clear that the upcoming leaders were mature and stable. By this time, there were several Bible schools within the country, supervised by several different missionaries. The goal was for the leadership to all be indigenous, but some of the nationals were not seasoned in ministry yet. Like everything else on the mission field, it would take time to establish them.

Soon a new missionary family came to Tomohon, the Eldon and Frances Browns, out of Washington state. They had a daughter, Barbara, who was close in age to Patsy. The two became fast friends. Barb's mother made wonderful fudge and taught the girls how to make it. Patsy often bicycled down to her end of town, or Barb would visit the Carlbloms; and together they did all the things teen-age girls do: listening to popular music on a radio station from the Philippines and dreaming of all the things they would someday like to do or become. God was good in giving Patsy another friend, as Loesje had moved with her family to another island.

Another change—a significant one—came upon their return to Tomohon. The Carlbloms rented a different house to be closer to the church. It was smaller than the previous one, with three rooms running side by side along an enclosed hall that had windows. One of the rooms was Jean and Harold's bedroom, and one was Charlaine and Marj's room. The third one they used as a living room. Patsy's room was actually a separate building outside the main part of the house, about 20 feet away. Because of past experiences, Harold rigged up a bell alarm system, so if she was afraid or heard intruders, she could buzz her parents immediately.

Patsy, Barbara, and Marjorie.

"Although I projected a brave front at being separated from the rest of the family, it was scary being out there by myself in the dark. Every night I read Psalm 91 to give me courage; and before I knew it, I had memorized it."
—Patsy

The bathroom and kitchen quarters were in a third building in the back, along with the servants' bedrooms. This building also housed the laundry, such as it was. Of course, they had no appliances for washing or drying, but the hired girls used washboards and tubs to clean the clothes.

The storage rooms were there as well, where they kept drums of supplies. Unfortunately, this was also the rats' territory. Rats were always a problem in Indonesia, and Jean sometimes did battle with them out there while she was digging in the drums for something or other—swinging a broom in an attempt to reduce their population. She took it all in stride, however, writing her mother, "We had a merry chase with a rat again today! I had to have someone help me corner him!"

Living in a home consisting of three buildings led to additional challenges. One example came in April 1956 when Harold was gone on a trip to one of the other islands as part of his duties. While he was gone, Patsy ended up sleeping in the main part of the house with Jean, in order to feel more secure with the rest of the family. One night during Harold's absence, an intruder broke into her room in the separate building and stole a lot of Patsy's clothes and a little jewelry box.

"The thing I was most sad about losing was a little plastic locket with a picture of Bob in it." —Patsy

After the intrusion, Jean and Harold didn't feel it was safe for Patsy to be separate from the rest of the family, and she moved into the main part of the house with her two younger sisters. They considered building on a couple of rooms to make more space but hesitated to do it because the house was just rented. However, they worked it out with the landlady to have it built and apply the cost to their rent.

It was a special treat for Jean to be able to decorate the new living room and dining room. For the first time since they had come to Indonesia as missionaries, she was able to choose the color of her walls and drapes.

She had always patiently accepted the far-less-than-perfect places with the attitude, "Well, we're just missionaries, so we'll make do." Perhaps the most exciting part of the new addition was an indoor bathroom to replace the outdoor toilets they'd always had. No more rats going down the hole and scaring Patsy out of the outhouse!

The addition made it an L-shaped house. It was in a quiet area of town, with the sounds of light traffic on the street. With few windows and homes open to the air, the typical sounds of life filtered throughout the neighborhood: babies crying, mothers calling for children, cooking, families coming together at the end of the day—it was a nice place to live.

Even though their housing situation had improved dramatically, medical and dental care was sometimes a problem. Jean experienced a terrible toothache for a number of days, and finally had to be taken down to Manado, the larger city down the mountain road, to have an infection lanced. The children did not see any dentists regularly while in Tomohon, because of the lack of good dentistry in remote areas. There was a Dutch doctor there who provided good medical care, but they didn't go to the doctor unless there was a serious condition. One illness came from a surprising source—surprising to Patsy, at any rate.

> "I can remember sitting on the front steps in the sunshine, listening to the clop-clop of a horse cart going by on the street, hearing the creaking of a pail being pulled up from the well, feeling at peace with the world, and thinking that I would always remember that moment, that feeling of contentment." —Patsy

She and her friend Barbara enjoyed stopping at a little food stand between their houses to eat *gado-gado*, an Indonesian salad.

The Brown family: Barb, Francis, Sandy, and Bill.

"Barbara, you're going to get sick eating at places like that!" her mother scolded her.

However, Barbara and Patsy still stopped at the vendor—and Barb just didn't tell her mom.

Eventually Patsy started experiencing fatigue and a low fever; and when her parents took her to the Dutch doctor, he diagnosed her with jaundice and blamed it on eating at a place that wasn't clean. However, in Indonesia at that time, there were no standards of cleanliness in any eating establishments, so it could have been from anywhere. They were given instructions for her not to eat anything with fats in it, and she recovered within a couple weeks. As ever, the family trusted that they were in God's hands.

Some issues weren't so difficult to deal with for Jean, who usually sat with both Marj and Charlaine to go through their schoolwork lessons. One morning she noticed something unusual. Marj's memory tells it well: "Mom kept listening, as though she were hearing something strange. Finally she asked, 'What is that squeaking noise?'

I said, 'Oh, you mean this?' I pulled a couple of baby mice out of my pocket. I had been carrying them around ever since Charlaine and I had found a nest of baby mice!"

While Jean had to deal with the everyday family issues like dentists and doctors, and mice, other discouragements came along the way in the realm of missionary work. In her many letters, Jean would sometimes tell her mother about these things and ask her to be praying for them. There were many things Harold had to address within the different churches. Sometimes young pastors did not address problems within their congregations or put forth effort in personal visitation when needed, and Harold had to provide encouragement and advice—and sometimes correction.

At times there were even accusations of questionable behavior, which Harold would have to sort through to find the truth. If you think of any given church you might know of, with the problems that exist within them, you could know that those problems exist to a greater extent in younger churches without proven leadership. And there was opposition, sometimes from the Islamic population. This could be a lot of noise outside to interfere with the services, intimidation of attenders by others standing outside the meeting, and threatening those who attended services. Often, though, the conflict originated from the established Protestant churches in the area or even from another Pentecostal church.

> *Last night I didn't go to the meeting, but the children, Patsy, and Barbara, went with Harold. Barbara plays an accordion. There has been good interest and attention in this place, and then last night this "Pinkster Kirk" [Dutch for Pentecostal Church], the other Pentecostal group from Seattle, had a meeting right next door, and the houses practically touch. So we just didn't have a meeting.*

One location where they held meetings was only about 15 miles away, but it took an hour to reach. The roads were so poor that they had to travel at about ten miles per hour.

One night, people were smoking, even though the missionaries had asked that people not smoke during the meeting. However, some troublemakers stood outside, close to the door, purposely blowing smoke into the building. Again they were asked not to smoke, but they continued doing it.

Then they started throwing stones into the building—three times! One large stone about the size of an apple hit a little five-year old girl very near the temple. The cut bled badly, and her face and dress were covered in blood.

The missionaries stopped the meeting to pray for the child, and God answered their prayers, as she was not seriously hurt. She was taken home to be cleaned up, bandaged, and changed, and then returned to the meeting.

No matter what the challenges were, the Carlbloms and the other missionaries continued to persevere. So much work was needed. By this time there were four missionary families in Tomohon: Harold and Jean Carlblom, Leonard and Mary Jane Lanphear, Morris (son of Ralph Devin) and Joyce Devin, and Bill and Frances Brown. It was decided that, because there were so many other needy areas of the country, two of the families should relocate. The Browns moved to the island of Ambon, where there was already a Bible school; and Jean and Harold moved to East Java, initially to help in a Bible school in Malang, and eventually to hold campaigns to establish new churches in that area of the very populous island.

In May of 1957, the Carlblom family made the move to East Java, and that same month, Patsy flew back to the States to be in her sister Joanne and Dick's wedding. Jean's grandma Low had passed away in April, and Patsy would be living with Jean's parents to finish her last year of high school in an American school. Again, Jean had losses in her life, with another of her daughters leaving before she turned 16, along with the loss of friends and connections in the Minahasa area where they had lived for a number of years. She wrote to her sister:

> *We surely miss our little Patsy. She made so many decisions with me and we talked things over together. Every time we go anywhere, I say, "Oh, I wish Patsy could have come here with us."*

Then for a time, the Carlbloms stayed in West Java, as there was a revival meeting there with an evangelist from the U.S., Harvey McAlister. Harold served as his interpreter. After the revival meetings, they began holding services in small villages nearby. They were so encouraged when it was clear their efforts were fruitful. One of Jean's letters recounts that God was moving through healings, and a number of the converts had been Muslim.

> *The man who was healed and his wife were formerly Muslim, as was the man who witnessed to him. They are so very enthusiastic. She told us the other night, "I am so very, very happy all the time. I never knew one could be so happy." She got several sisters and a brother saved, and the one sister who brought us to her village home last week is busy going door to door each day telling people about the Lord. She takes her Bible and asks them to read. One man asked, "This is wonderful—is it true?" She said, "Yes," and showed him more, and he was amazed and asked if he could take*

this book to show it to his relatives. He had some sick relatives who would want to hear. So she let him take it. She testified to another lady until one in the morning, then the next morning this second lady brought her sick mother and asked her to tell her this good news; and the mother came to our service. After service that night, in which we had prayed for quite a number, she talked to a neighbor till one or two in the morning. When we took our walk through the "kampung" [village], we met all the people whom we had prayed for, healed and working—either drawing water or working in the field or their yards. It was so thrilling. It is so encouraging to watch the enthusiasm of these people. They are always coming with pleas like, "I went over to such and such a village and told the people there about the Lord, and there are about twenty there who want you to come for meetings." When we were here a few weeks ago, we held meetings in one of these places and now in another. Last time it rained almost every night and we had to walk quite a way through a terribly muddy road to reach the house. It was slippery mud, and when we got there, we looked a sight, but they gave us a knife to clean off our shoes a little.

Eventually they returned to East Java, to the city of Malang, which is about a two-hour journey from the large city of Surabaya. It was in the mountains, supposedly cooler, but it would still get in the nineties often. Because rentals were so difficult to find, the family stayed in the church in Malang. Since this was a temporary location, one of the difficulties Jean had was knowing what to unpack from the drums they had shipped from the States. Typical things packed in drums were drapes or curtains, blankets, clothing for all family members, toilet paper, linens, Sunday school material, canned goods, books, and other miscellaneous items. They were not packed in such a way to be organized by rooms or types. Belongings were mixed up, arranged to protect breakable things while still making good use of the space. So when Jean went to unpack things she needed temporarily, she had to dig around in several drums to find what was needed, then repack what she had no room for at the time.

Since Harold was serving as the superintendent and didn't have the responsibilities of teaching in Bible school, he had more time to visit some of the churches, and he also served as interpreter whenever an evangelist from the States would visit Indonesia. He had become fluent in the Indonesian language, and when he interpreted for visiting speakers, he put a lot of feeling and enthusiasm into it. He wanted so much for the listeners to take the gospel message to heart. Harold wrote of their burden for the people of Indonesia in a form letter in September of 1957.

> *Bandung was also the place for an All Indonesia Preachers' Conference, with such well-known and deeply respected men as Dr. Bob Pierce, Dr. Paul Rees of Minneapolis, [Minnesota], Rev. Harold Jefferies of Portland, [Oregon], and other fine men as the team who ministered. Bob Pierce was the promoter of this unusual effort for God, and he as well as his teammates were made a real blessing to the more than 600 ministers and lay-workers who assembled there, with World Vision paying all expenses. It was a most wonderful time, and we all came away wishing that our entire group of ministers could have been there!*
>
> *Now we are "home" again in Malang and engaged in evangelistic meetings here. There is such a need for evangelism all over these islands! As we have now driven across Java several times, our hearts have been deeply impressed and burdened as we have seen these millions of people without Christ! Here lies one of the world's most densely populated areas! It is a mighty challenge to us here. Will you continue to pray for us as we endeavor to obey His commission?*

During 1958, they stayed in Bandung, East Java, living in the home of missionaries Fred and Cathy McGrew while the McGrews were on furlough. Rentals were so difficult to come by that when one of the missionary families would go home to the U.S. on furlough, another family would take over their home for the year they were gone in order to retain the rental of a suitable property. When the missionary returned, another family would be ready for furlough. Therefore, since Harold was traveling to different churches and pastors as part of his ministry as superintendent, he and Jean moved frequently, living in several different areas. When they moved to Bandung, Marjorie and Charlaine were able to attend school at the Christian Missionary Alliance School, which freed up Jean's time to help Harold with visitation after campaigns. Besides, it was good for Marj and Charlaine to have more socialization.

During this time, evangelist Harold Herman came to hold services, and—as usual—Harold Carlblom served as his interpreter. The buildings they had rented were filled from the start, and they had to move to larger quarters in each of the cities. In Bandung, where the assembly was just a handful of people, God drew from every place and filled the building. Around 3,000 came forward and signed decision cards during the campaign, and many attendees reported healings.

After each campaign, Jean and Harold were tireless in visitation, often going into the inner parts of the city called *kampungs*, (neighborhoods) where little lanes led this way and that. The couple walked long distances, finding their way to tiny homes that represented souls for God. People who accepted Christ during a campaign filled out a card with their information, and sometimes it was difficult for Jean and Harold to find the places;

but they spent day after day walking in the heat of the day to find the people and encourage them as they started walking with the Lord. Often it was this extra effort to meet the people where they lived that brought them back to the church again and again.

When the missionaries traveled longer distances, from one end of Java to the other, they usually took the train, as roads were not good, and car travel took far longer. The trains were generally crowded, and sometimes Jean and Harold ended up standing—unless they went to the dining car. In that case, they'd make their food last as long as possible in order to be able to sit. Once they arrived in their destination city, transportation was always available on bicycle-driven *becas*.

No matter where they went, they felt the presence of God. Jean told her mother in a letter that it seemed there was something encouraging in almost every service: an answer to prayer, a healing, or a testimony from someone. One woman's little granddaughter in Djakarta got whooping cough and was very sick. She started choking, and began turning black. They called a doctor nearby who said there was no hope. But a neighbor came to rush her to the hospital.

Charlaine and Marjorie in bicycle-driven beca (with a couple of hitchhikers).

The grandmother said to them, "Oh, if only Brother Carlblom were here, he would pray, and she would be all right!" But then, as she told them later, "He wasn't there, so I prayed myself—I didn't care who heard me—I just got down and prayed out loud. My daughter and son didn't know how to pray."

When they got to the hospital, the child began to move, and the blackness left her skin. She was okay! They examined her anyhow, but she was all right. This event had a powerful effect in their lives and in the lives of their family.

Jean told of another family in one of her letters:

Did we tell you about the Tan family? He was very, very sick, and his neighbors had been testifying to him and offered to call their preacher to pray for him. We went, and God helped him. A few weeks later a tragedy struck them. Their 20-year-old daughter, disappointed in love, drank poison and died suddenly. Harold was asked to take the funeral. The end of that week, they called us to the home, and there they sat—the whole family in a circle, while the father told us that they had thrown away all their idols and anything pertaining to ancestor worship and the other customs they followed. They said, "We want you to tell us about the gospel—we want to be Christians." One couldn't keep back the tears. How touching it was, as Harold talked to them and explained salvation, to see the mother and father sitting with tears, and the older children very soberly listening and nodding in assent showing they were accepting it all. Then we prayed. The two girls, ages 19 and 21, hadn't slept well the whole week because of terrible dreams. We prayed especially that they would sleep and the mother could sleep and not be bothered with asthma. The next day we saw them at church, and both girls and the mother had slept all night. We just found out a couple of days ago that the man also gave up smoking when he threw out all his idols. The neighbor who testified to them had smoked for 61 years—since he was eight years old—and was a very heavy smoker; and he has been delivered in the last couple of weeks. So, God is still working; we are making new contacts and seeing progress in the lives of these people all the time.

Knowing that their efforts were indeed making a difference for the people of their adopted country, the Carlbloms returned to the States in July of 1959 for their furlough. They rented the upstairs of the house owned by a family from the Minneapolis Gospel Tabernacle, and Patsy moved back in with them after a semester at North Central Bible College. They attended a General Council of the Assemblies of God in San Antonio shortly after getting back. Their year was kept busy visiting churches that supported them.

But this year would be a very difficult one for Jean and Harold.

Harold had been accused of being hard to work with; the reproach came along with a number of other grievances by several of the other missionaries in a letter of complaint to the headquarters in Springfield. The timing was less than ideal—right after the Carlbloms had gone back to the U.S. on furlough—so they had no chance to discuss the issues and work through the problems, even though they had just been with the other missionaries at the annual conference.

Missionaries are just as human as everyone else: sometimes critical, sometimes jealous, sometimes unfair, maybe proprietary about their individual areas of responsibility. Harold may have been difficult to work with at times, as he had definite ideas of how things should be done. And he showed his emotions quickly. He could have been described as quick-tempered. Nevertheless, this accusation seemed to be calculated in its timing, and it came without specifics.

Letters supporting the Carlbloms from Indonesian leaders, expressing great appreciation for their ministry also arrived in Springfield. Through this process, Springfield acknowledged that Indonesia was a mission field like no other, in that missionaries were spread across many islands with only letters to connect them, and there was a tendency for the missionaries to operate independently. Letters sent among headquarters, the other missionaries, and the Carlbloms show that the main office in Springfield was not about to call them back from the mission field unless there was substantiation of the complaints, and they urged all the missionaries to work together in harmony.

Harold and Jean experienced the most discouraging time of their missionary career during this year, but to their credit, because of God's grace and forgiveness working in them, they put the past behind them and prepared to return to the field.

Years later, one of the missionaries who was behind the complaint wrote to Harold, "I want you to know that I, for one, want you and Jean to come back to the field. I feel that the Lord has used and blessed your ministry in Central Java, and that you are a very valuable asset to this field. Your ministry is needed. It is my feeling that you have the calling to this type of work, and that very few, (if any) of the other missionaries on the field could do the work you have been doing."

By the summer of 1960, Patsy started dating a very special guy from the church named Bob Pearson, whom she had known and had a crush on when she was fourteen years old during the family's furlough. It didn't take long for the two of them to know they were meant to be together; and by Christmas, Bob had put an engagement ring on Patsy's finger!

Jean and Harold were preparing to go back to Indonesia shortly after the holidays. Since the young couple didn't want to wait four years to get married—and they couldn't quite put together a wedding in several weeks—this would mean Jean and Harold wouldn't be able to be present for their second daughter's wedding, either. Possibly this was part of the reason Jean had such a difficult time when they left for Indonesia in mid-January. She wrote her mother:

> *When we left, I felt I had so little time to talk and to kiss you and Barb. But if we'd had more time, we'd only have cried. I tried not to cry till after I was on the plane. Every time I thought of you all, I'd just sob. Then I calmed down, and a lady asked, "Are you going away or going home?" And again I cried. Another asked later "How long will you be gone?"—and I started again. It was so hard this time. I turned back to search for you as we walked out and couldn't see you or Barb.*

Chapter 8

Planting Churches in Central Java: Fourth Term

Do your best to present yourself to God as one approved, a worker who does not need to be ashamed and who correctly handles the word of truth. —2 Timothy 2:15

Returning to Indonesia in early 1961, Jean and Harold first went to Bandung in West Java and then made a six-hour trip by train to Djokjakarta, in Central Java, to see the possibilities for a campaign there. Jean wrote:

> *Here is something for the books. We got to our hotel at 11:00 a.m. No sheets on the bed, and when questioned, they responded, "Very sorry, 'Tuan' [Mister], but this is rainy season and they aren't dry—this afternoon." After dinner we wanted a nap. No sheets, so we asked again, and he came back with some sheets and said, "They've just been used a few times, or maybe just once, Tuan." But Tuan refused. Sometimes it does no good. We took naps without sheets! And now it's 8:00 p.m. and still no sheets!*

This city in Central Java is variously known as Djokjakarta, Jogjakarta in more recent years, or Yogyakarta. It's is a thriving, busy city, which was briefly the capital of Indonesia when Djakarta was occupied by the Dutch. It has now been given the status of a special district.

The Carlbloms moved to Djokjakarta, also shortened to Djokja, by the middle of April. In August they conducted an evangelistic campaign there and established the Djokja church and a Bible school. Foster and Louise Woods, another missionary couple, came to help with the Bible school and church planting. Jean and Harold had a very difficult time finding a house in this area. There was very little available to rent, and if they did find something, the rents were high.

Harold had received funding from the U.S. to build or buy land for the Bible school, and he converted the money into Indonesian rupiahs. A delay occurred, and the rupiah's value happened to be falling at that time, so he bought gold bullion, which would retain its value.

It was difficult to find a place to hold services also. In Djokja they rented a room for the campaign in a building where they had to cross through a number of other rooms used for a variety of purposes such as dance instruction, ping-pong, pool, and gaming. Though they had been assured there would always be electricity, often they had none, so they resorted to bringing portable lighting.

The local police complicated the matter, extracting a cost for a police permit. Then there was a permit for taking offerings. The second week they made a new requirement: collecting the names and addresses of all the people who were prayed for. The third week they also needed to know the names of the sicknesses that people were prayed for. Next the police demanded that Harold send in every sermon he had used, written in full.

The missionaries felt a real resistance from the powers of darkness, even sometimes sensing difficulty in praying. At the end of the fourth week, when they were done using this location for nightly services, there was a drama production in that very room about black magic, advertised by a sign with a caricature of the devil, hoping to capture some of the attendance that there had been for their services. Despite the efforts of Satan, on the closing night of the campaign, half the audience came forward for the altar call. God was faithful! Jean and Harold were glad to be able to use the building twice a week after the campaign, on Sunday mornings and Wednesday evenings.

Up to this point during this term in Indonesia, they had made do without a car, as there had been complications. Sometimes a missionary would leave their car in storage in order to be used during the next term. However, quite often it just wasn't practical, as they had to find a place to leave it where it would be safe; and after the hard use on difficult roads for several years, it often wasn't worth it. Cars were easily resold at the end of a term. So when an agent of the Holden car company in Australia quoted Harold a price that met his budget, Harold pursued it. The car company backtracked, saying they couldn't give him that price, as it was just for diplomats.

Harold wrote back, "Although I could not be classified as a diplomat, I am in service for the King of Kings, the Lord Jesus Christ. This car will be used for His work." They wrote back that, after considering his comments, they would sell him the car at the price quoted for diplomats!

In 1962, another church was established in the Central Java area in the city of Solo. It started with a campaign in a Chinese hall. Between 500 and 750 people responded to the altar calls. The typical pattern for a church start was a city-wide campaign, followed by laborious follow-up and visitation. The Bible school students were also a great help in this, but Jean and Harold were tireless workers, leading the way.

Also during that year, they received the sad news that Harold's mom, Anna Carlblom, had passed away after long years of having diabetes and then a stroke, which eventually led to her death. At that time, missionaries were not permitted to travel to the States for anything during a term unless it was at their own expense. As always, money was tight, so Jean and Harold were not able to go.

One of Jean's letters in 1962 tells about the terrible fatigue Harold was feeling. Their busy schedule included services in a town that was an hour away by car. Driving in Indonesia at that time was very taxing. Oxcart and bicycle traffic along with car traffic with very few rules of the road made driving strenuous. And then when they arrived at the place of the services, there was, of course, no air conditioning in the tropical heat. When Harold preached, he put everything into it—he was soaked in perspiration by the end. As always, he pushed on.

In the fall of 1962, they began a campaign in Klaten, a city about a half hour away. Jean reported many healings during this campaign, along with many who received salvation. God blessed in the meetings and provided a good nucleus of people for the new congregation.

Another year had passed, and Marjorie, their third daughter, went back to the U.S. in the early part of 1963. After a couple weeks staying with Jean's parents and sister Barb, she moved to Fond du Lac, Wisconsin, to live with her oldest sister, Joanne, and brother-in-law Dick. Dick and Jo pastored a church of the Fellowship of Independent Assemblies. It wasn't too long before a young man named Bob Liebelt asked Marjorie out, and they began dating. The reader may remember that, many years before, Jean and Harold had held evangelistic services in that city—and in the church Jo and Dick were pastoring . . . and that they had even stayed with one of the Liebelt families!

In May of 1963, with only Charlaine still in the country with them, Harold and Jean held another campaign in Muntilan, near Magelang, towns about a half hour from where they were living in Djokja. When they inquired about the police permit again, they were informed that the office had no paper—and that Jean and Harold would need to supply the paper for the permits!

They came up with some paper, and their work went on; and they had good results—with great responses on altar calls for salvation and for healing. However, the enemy was working against them. They had been promised the ability to use a certain building twice a week following the campaign, but the deal fell through. Lead after lead on other possibilities didn't work out. Someone would promise the use of a building, but the next day they would back out. But despite Satan's opposition, a hall was finally rented for the purpose of planting a church that would continue through the years.

In the midst of all of this work, tragedy struck again. Jean's beloved dad, "Granddaddy Ramsay" to the children, died in July of 1963; and, of course, Jean and Harold were not able to be with the rest of the family to celebrate his life. Granddaddy was loved by all who met him. Whenever someone came to visit him, he would embrace them and have a Pentecostal prayer meeting right then and there. One of the greatest joys of his life was to praise God. At his funeral, a friend commented, "I think when he made his entrance [to heaven] he said, 'Angels, move over, you have a little competition now.'"

Knowing that Granddaddy Ramsay was in God's hands, they continued on. A few months later, in

October 1963, they conducted a three-week campaign in Madiun, which drew more than 300 people over several nights. The campaign was quite successful, with many people coming to Christ, but Satan was still opposing.

On the closing night of the campaign, shortly before the service was to begin, as Harold drove down the narrow and twisting mountain road into the city, the brakes of his car failed—suddenly and completely!

He tried downshifting, but nothing was working.

He told the story later. "Ahead lay a continuous steep descent with many people in the roadway. The problem was where I should turn off the road. In a fleeting second, I saw the only place just ahead on the left. After that, there was no place! I started praying out loud, 'Oh God, help us,' and made for the left bank. It was almost a wall of dirt with rocks embedded in the bank. We jumped the ditch and hit with a grinding impact and started to climb it, but then the inevitable happened—we turned over on a three-quarter roll and stopped! Thank God it didn't go completely over, for we would have started rolling down the road again."

Harold crawled out the driver's window while someone asked for the keys and opened the back-end gate, so the passengers could get out. Aside from bumps and bruises, everyone was okay, and Harold made quick arrangements to take a taxi down the mountain to get to the service. They arrived at 7:20, and Harold was preaching by 7:30!

During this term of service, Jean and Harold, along with the help of Bible school students and missionaries Foster and Louise Woods, conducted campaigns and opened five churches in Central Java, a very populous area. They consistently experienced difficulties getting a hall to use for the campaign, and then again renting

A Balinese dancer.

Balinese girls taking fruit offerings to their temple.

something to be used after the campaign for regular church services.

April 1964 greeted the family with a telegram telling that Grampa Carlblom had passed away. So three of their four parents were gone. The situation was truly disheartening. One of the things that missionaries at that time really missed was being with other family members at a time of grieving. Grief shared heals the heart, and to be so distant from family was very difficult, especially before the days of email, texts, and video calls. Today the Assemblies of God missions department has built-in funds for these situations, so missionaries can take emergency trips home for family crises like that—and that's a healthy thing. Sadly, the Carlbloms didn't have that option, but they knew they were in God's will, in His hands. They persevered.

The middle of 1965 was the time they were scheduled for furlough. Their daughter Joanne and son-in-law Dick visited them in Indonesia prior to their leaving. They were able to visit some of the churches with Jean and Harold, as well as the island of Bali. Like always, bad roads (a flooded one!) meant car trouble.

After that trip, the Balkens and the Carlbloms all returned to the U.S. through Europe, visiting several countries before arriving in New York on August 10.

After getting back to Minnesota, Jean and Harold met their new Pearson grandson, Steven Kent, for the first time. They delighted in spending time with baby Stevie, almost a year old, as he began talking. They also enjoyed time with Brenton and Byron Balken, Joanne and Dick's boys, in Fond du Lac. Spending so much time away from their grandkids, they made the most of the time they had on furlough.

"We boarded a ferry, taking our car with us to the island. At one point in our travel around the island, we came to a place where a river was washing over the road. We saw buses parked on the other side, and Dad asked some men if the buses had gone across and if it was safe to drive across the flooded road. They said it was. As we started driving across, the water got deeper and the engine stalled. Dad jumped out of the car and asked the men to help push it to the other side. They responded with an exorbitant price, and Dad began arguing with them. When the water in the car kept rising, I jumped out of the car, thinking my chances of survival were better outside the car than in it. Suddenly I realized Dad was no longer there! About 20 minutes later, Dad appeared with an official from town who helped negotiate a price with the men, who eventually pushed us out of the river. For the remainder of the trip we had trouble with the waterlogged engine." —Charlaine

In October Marjorie married Bob Liebelt, surrounded by her family. All her sisters were in the wedding party, and having her parents present for the glad occasion was truly a blessing.

As the furlough drew to a close, Harold and Jean took a trip to Banff, Alberta, Canada, with their daughters, sons-in-law, and the three grandsons in August of 1966. The family made great memories hiking, horseback riding, sightseeing, and mountain climbing. Harold, with Charlaine and Bob Pearson climbed the majestic Mount Rundle, but the rest of the family was content to climb the lower elevations!

Along with making memories with the family, Jean and Harold were also preparing to leave their youngest daughter Charlaine behind. She would be living in the apartment they were vacating, along with several friends, so this time it would just be Jean and Harold going back to Indonesia.

Chapter 9

Just the Two of Them Again: Fifth Term

When anxiety was great within me, your consolation brought me joy. —Psalm 94:19

Just before Christmas of 1966, Jean and Harold flew back to Indonesia—for the first time, it was just the two of them. Harold jumped right in, preaching a service in Djakarta the day after they arrived. Unfortunately, they found tense conditions in the country, with many opposed to President Sukarno, who was closely associated with the Communist Party of Indonesia. There had been a short-lived attempted coup on October 1, 1965; and in the ensuing vigilante action, it was estimated that half a million people were killed. By March of 1966, Major General Suharto had taken over authority from President Sukarno.

By the time the Carlbloms returned, much had changed. Thousands of students demonstrated against Sukarno and the Communist Party. The island of Java was divided in their loyalties, with West Java being anti-Sukarno, and East Java standing with him. During the demonstrations, incidents of cars being stolen or vandalized were common, so Jean and Harold took to keeping their car in a rented garage.

During this problematic time, mail was routinely opened and censored, so Jean and Harold devised a code they could use in communication with their family back in the U.S., as well as numbering their letters to make sure all were getting through. In addition, whenever other missionaries were traveling out of the country, they would hand carry letters that spoke plainly about conditions and mail them outside the country. Otherwise, they had to be very neutral in their observations of what was happening—or their letters would be confiscated.

Times were strange, but some things never seemed to change—like riding the Indonesian trains. If Harold and Jean were traveling from East Java to West Java, they usually took the train because it was faster than traveling by car on the bad roads. Jean wrote to her grandmother, describing this unusual and sometimes risky experience.

> *The trains are so crowded that there are folks filling the aisles with their suitcases, and maybe some chickens tied up, sacks of vegetables. And often they sit on these things; but if they have children, those spots are taken by the children, so they will sit on the armrest of your seat.*
>
> *Everyone seems to stop their work and look at the trains except those with loads on their backs or heads. We pass rice fields that always have workers in them. We passed a number of places where they were making bricks. Some were laid out to dry, and others were stacked up, and they were already making a fire underneath them that will burn several days to dry them out completely.*
>
> *We passed a group of children who stopped their play and waved to the train—it's the same the world over—a train fascinates people. We passed bridges where people sat watching the train but with their hind ends sticking out over the stream taking care of morning needs.*
>
> *We passed a home that was open so we could see the dirt floor inside with a child crawling on it. Another*

mother walked along a dike, the ridge of earth around the edge of each rice paddy, with a load on her head and a tiny girl right behind her with a load on her head also.

When Harold and Jean traveled by train, it was a great stress to keep their bags safe from theft. One time when they were taking the train from Djokja to Surabaya, they left Djokja at 4:00 a.m. The train was crowded even at that early hour, and the crush intensified all along the way.

Arriving at the first station in Surabaya, Harold decided on a proactive approach.

"We'd better move toward the end of the car with all of this luggage. Our stop is a short one—about five minutes, and I don't know if we'd make our way through the crowd in that time if we stay put."

Jean saw the wisdom in his plan, but this would be a difficult maneuver. People were pushing—both coming and going—making it hard even to stand in the packed aisle. Harold grasped two cases, one on top of the other—with one hand covering the top case and one hand holding a small item underneath. And besides, that? The manual typewriter tucked under his arm. Jean, ever vigilant, had set the briefcase down at her feet between them so she could keep an eye on his billfold pocket, her purse tucked tightly under her arm with the strap tucked securely underneath so no one could grab it. In the end, they disembarked with all their baggage, but when they got to the hotel, Jean was in for a surprise. She looked at her black patent purse and saw that it had been slit in several places with a razor.

Another time, on a train trip to Djokja, they had set their cases on a rack right above their seats. Just as they were pulling into the station, Harold stood to gather their things. He started with the smaller items, handing them down to Jean. Finally, he reached for the larger case, which had been there a moment before—but it was gone!

Harold started for the exit with a holler, "Someone took my case—where is my case?"

Everyone nearby could hear the commotion, and by the time he struggled out the car, whoever had taken the case had also dropped it—just in front of the steps leading off the train. There it was—safe and sound with all its contents. What a relief—this piece of luggage held Harold's cameras, which they'd been told never to carry out where they could be seen. It was a moment to give thanks and realize once more—they were in God's care.

In a country like Indonesia where poverty is rampant, perhaps it's inevitable that theft is such a problem. Taking precautions at every turn, they still had problems. It was common for missionaries to ship supplies in drums—welded shut. Even when taking this amount of care, one of the missionary families found their welded drums broken into. In fact, two out of their four drums had been completely emptied, and the other two were almost empty.

Even mailing letters was difficult. The Carlbloms always tried to use post offices they trusted, as sometimes the stamps were removed from the envelopes and the letters never got through. They took to personally carrying their mail to their trusted post office; but they also requested the stamped letters to be hand cancelled in front of them, as a cancelled stamp would have no value to someone wanting to steal it.

The new year began with blessed news: In January 1967, another boy was added to the list of grandchildren. Scott Liebelt's birth made a total of four grandsons. Jean and Harold also gained a new foster granddaughter, Eydie, whom Joanne and Dick had brought into their family as a teenager.

In the first week of April came a turn for the worse. Harold was heading down from Malang to Surabaya to check on another shipment of drums that had finally arrived. The roads and traffic being what they were, he was involved in a serious accident. The car was badly damaged, and Harold was left with serious injury to his kneecap and surrounding tendons. Truly, it was only through God's providence that Jean hadn't accompanied him, for the damage on her side of the car was far more serious. Looking at how the vehicle was crushed, it was clear that—had Jean been sitting in the passenger's seat—she would have been badly injured, or even killed. Harold's kneecap was fractured, and he had many bumps and bruises. He was hospitalized for a week and a half, then wore a cast for two weeks, which slowed him down quite a bit. For many weeks afterward, he faithfully did his therapy exercises. The long recovery time wasn't easy. It was really hard for Harold to be slowed down this way.

His injury came at an especially inconvenient time, as they were just about to move into a rented house and still had to get their drums cleared through customs. With Harold's "Let's get it done!" attitude, it must have been a patience-building exercise. For over four weeks straight, he daily asked the customs office workers when his drums would be cleared; and each time they'd reply, "Tomorrow," but the next day he'd receive the same answer.

They finally got into their house at the end of May and got their drums released from customs. Jean worked like fury to get everything unpacked. Jean and Harold were quite conservative in the number of drums they'd brought out, only 12. Many of the other missionaries had brought 20 or 30. Jean sometimes expressed a wish that she had brought along one thing or another, but on the whole, they were quite careful about what they brought along. And so, they managed without. It seems they didn't want to live so far above the people to whom they ministered.

By June, Harold was still doing his exercises for an hour a day—and still tiring out easily after exerting himself. But when he saw a Baptist doctor who was a bone specialist, the doctor said Harold was doing well. The encouragement came with a side note, that he might experience swelling for up to a year. Even so, Harold's natural inclination to push himself as far as he could no doubt helped him to heal.

With or without a bum knee, their schedule was taxing. Harold and Jean each taught four hours of classes in the Malang Bible School on Monday and Tuesday, so they had to drive up to two hours to get there, depending on the traffic. Then, when they returned home in Surabaya on Tuesday afternoon, they held a service late that afternoon—and services every other evening of the week. They also did extensive visitation the rest of the week, sometimes from early in the morning until nightfall. Jean described it to her mom in a letter.

> *I wish you could have been with us on some of these visits. I see it all the time, but never cease to be moved by the poverty and sickness and filth. We have so much in comparison.*
>
> *We went in one tiny little place where the room was so small that sitting together, our knees were all touching each other. The bed took up the full width of the room and one of our group sat there, another sat on a low*

stool, the lady sat on a pile of stuff covered by a cloth and gave me the only chair she had. It was a lean-to room on a different house, which wasn't much better. It had woven bamboo walls through which you could see the light from outside, partly covered with newspapers or brown wrapping paper, the thin kind that tears so easily, but it would maybe keep the wind out on a rainy night. She had a page torn out of a magazine with President Lyndon Johnson's picture and was so proud of that part of her wall. With a smile on her face and a dreamy look in her eyes, she said, "When I get to heaven I will have a mansion," and went on describing that place with joy almost as if she were musing to herself and not conscious of our presence there; then with a laugh she came back to earth and said, "But I just have a shack here. I'm so glad you would come to see me in this old place."

I asked if it leaked when it rained, because we do have such hard rains, you know. And she said, "Oh yes, I sit right there in that chair all night. I roll my bed cover to the end and cover it with plastic, and then sit in that chair because it is the only spot that doesn't leak."

As they continued to minister to those living in abject poverty—and living in less-than-ideal conditions themselves, another grandchild came at the end of 1967. Kristin Noelle was born to Bob and Patsy Pearson. How exciting! Jean and Harold would have a baby granddaughter to love and cherish. They received lots of photos to enjoy—and show others!

In January of 1968, The Carlbloms were able to take a much-needed vacation. They got away to a beach resort in Singapore and truly had time to relax. While they were out of Indonesia, they freely wrote home of the situation there:

There is a growing feeling of hatred of the Muslims toward the Christians. There was an open letter written by a member of Parliament to the President by a Muslim. He was rabid in his criticisms and revealed a terrible hatred. He said that maybe the time had come for another Holy War, the War of the Sword. It came because of the progress of Christianity since the coup. So in a country 90% Muslim, one doesn't know what could happen. If Islam became a state religion, our work might be over.

After this letter, in Makassar (Ujung Pandang) there was an incident that stirred the Muslims to attack every church and religious school in one night. Hartimedes is our pastor there, and he was ready to send his wife back to Minahasa. There have been other incidents here and there. In Borneo a whole group of young Chinese Christians were killed—brutally murdered as they held a jungle service."

The problems simmered for a while, and then seemed to die down, but an underlying tension still existed.

Evangelist Gene Martin, who had held campaigns in Indonesia, raised funds along with Kathryn Kuhlman in the U.S. for a new church building in Surabaya. This building opened in November of 1968, accompanied by a four-week campaign with evangelist Hal Herman. Later campaigns with Gene Martin and Eddie Wilson helped to build the congregation, and Jean and Harold engaged in systematic follow-up of all converts. During one of Eddie Wilson's campaigns, the Sunday school reached 1,100 one Sunday. They were able to stabilize with about 600 regular attendees in Sunday school. Other evangelists and pastors who came for campaigns were John Hudson from the States and Yonggi Cho of Korea.

During this time, Jean and Harold were troubled by quite a few bouts of sickness. They sometimes wondered if it was partly due to Satanic attacks, but their schedule was also extremely busy, with very few letups, leaving their defenses low. Because they were in Surabaya, a travel hub, many evangelists and visitors coming into the country needed to be fetched from the airport and taken around to various churches—and also entertained with meals at Jean and Harold's. The same was true for missionaries coming from some of the outlying Indonesian islands. Through it all, they were still teaching two days a week in Malang, with that hour-and-a-half or two-hour drive. When there were special services, it was usually up to Harold to do the interpreting, which took a lot of energy. However, evangelists appreciated the way he entered into the tone of the message with great enthusiasm—and it was all about the mission—so he never questioned making the effort.

Jean came back to the States alone the middle of 1969 for six months, partly because of the declining health of her mother, and partly because she and Harold were very concerned about their daughter Charlaine, and the choices she was making. They felt that Jean might be a helpful influence on her. Jean enjoyed the visit with her mother and her daughter, and she was there to greet yet another granddaughter, Heidi Jo Balken, a little redhead, who was born in October to Joanne and Dick.

Half a year had never seemed so long to Harold without the love of his life by his side. He wrote letters to his "Dearest Jeannie" often, and in his journal, he counted down the days with many exclamation points till his "honey girl" was to come back! However, there was much work to keep him busy in East Java and Central Java.

In July he wrote,

> *Dearest Jeannie Girl,*
> *It is Monday morning and I'm sitting here with my ear tuned to the Voice of America [radio broadcast], and we are waiting for the astronauts to come out of their*

spaceship. I went to bed last night at 8:30 and set the alarm for 1:30 a.m. so that I could follow the descent to the moon. I felt this too momentous a moment to be sleeping it away!

The radio was essential for Harold. He wanted to keep in touch with what was going on around the world, but especially in the U.S. Sometimes he would even rise in the middle of the night to listen to an "important" football game!

He was able to golf at a nearby golf club and took advantage of it when he could; but it was not a leisurely day of golf for him the way one might imagine. He was usually on the course before 6:00 a.m., and he often finished 18 holes in less than two hours with a score in the high eighties.

Taking time to play or relax was a rarity, but in 1970, the couple enjoyed a new luxury. For the first time in their many years in a humid, tropical climate, they had an air conditioner unit in their home, one left behind by another missionary. What a blessing it was—and especially helpful to Harold, who was often bothered by heat rash.

Still stationed in Surabaya, in January they conducted a short campaign in Madiun in Central Java at a church that had been established in their previous term. February and March brought more meetings in Bandung and Tjimahi (now Cimahi) in West Java.

News came in the spring of 1970 when another granddaughter was born, Chère Liebelt, born to Marjorie and Bob. Having three granddaughters in a row would make for great fun when the family all gathered together in years to come.

The same year Jean and Harold also received news that Charlaine had married Jerry Cruncleton, from

Tulsa, Oklahoma. Once again, they were disappointed to be unable to travel home and participate in the special occasion and celebrate with their youngest daughter.

No matter what was happening in the U.S., the mission work continued. Harold and Jean took time off from Surabaya in April to start the church in Magelang, Central Java. They worked side by side with missionary Ray Trask and made it happen. The 500 chairs they'd rented were filled practically from the start. Hundreds came forward for salvation. A group of young men traveled on bicycles from sixty kilometers away to help with ushering and taking down names during the altar calls.

Magelang is situated among several volcanos near the ancient Buddhist temple of Borobudur. It is the largest Buddhist temple in the world, dating back to the eighth and ninth centuries. Borobudur was restored with the help of UNESCO (United Nations Educational, Scientific and Cultural Organization) over several years beginning in 1975. It is a historical site, not used for Buddhist ceremonies at the present, but it is a widely known tourist attraction. While the temple is not used now, the Carlbloms hoped and trusted that the churches they were establishing in Central Java would bring results for eternity.

June brought a campaign with evangelist Eddie Wilson. Harold had hoped to have the Wilson campaign sooner in the spring because of the busy summer schedule, but he didn't succeed in changing it. Thus, they plowed on. In July they packed in both the Missionary Conference and the National Church Congress. In August—and into September—came a major campaign in Djakarta. The schedule was overwhelming, but God was moving. Their hard work always seemed worth the effort.

However, by September 15, Jean and Harold found themselves unexpectedly in Minneapolis. Harold's voice was giving out, probably because of the intensive schedule. The diagnosis? Nodules on his overworked vocal cords, for which he underwent surgery that fall. Recovery wouldn't be easy for the man who accomplished much of his work with his voice. The surgery forced Harold to refrain from speaking for several weeks so he could recover. He communicated through notebooks.

The Carlbloms spent the rest of 1970 and much of the following year in the States, preparing for another term. By then, after two and a half decades, working in the mission field was simply a lifestyle for them, and there wasn't a question of whether or not to return to their beloved Indonesia. They only looked forward to what God had for them next.

Chapter 10

The Moluccan Islands: Sixth Term

If I rise on the wings of the dawn, if I settle on the far side of the sea, even there your hand will guide me, your right hand will hold me fast. —Psalm 139:9–10

In October 1971 Harold and Jean headed back to Indonesia for their sixth term of service. They made a trip to Ambon and other Moluccan Islands (also called the Spice Islands) in November for a ministers' seminar and evangelical services. They traveled by motorboat or outrigger canoe from one island to another. Once they arrived on an island, sometimes the only available transportation was their own feet. However, sometimes an old, rickety bus would take them from one village to another.

In one letter home, Jean described one bus this way:

> *They had to crank a long time to get going. When we started, it was so noisy. We never have been on such an old bus in all our twenty-five years out here. The hood had rusted through many places, and there were many holes. They poured a can of water in to cool the engine before starting. In a few blocks we were steaming and spouting out water, and they just threw an old gunny sack over it. When we came to a hill we just chugged and crawled.*
>
> *I was sitting with my legs over a hole in the bus floor next to the driver. When the trip was over, I found that my leg was sprayed with engine oil, and it felt like it was burning.*

The remote island roads had deep ruts, and the bus drivers would drive on the ridges between the ruts so undercarriage wouldn't drag. In one place a man had to get out and walk ahead of the bus to direct the driver atop the ridges. An even bigger concern than bottoming out? Slipping into the deep ruts and overturning the bus.

Getting aboard a motorboat to travel to another island wasn't any safer. It was typical to sleep on beds made only of boards—or even on the floor. And there were no mattresses, only thin mats, which provided little comfort and less cleanliness. The size of the watercraft made no difference when it came to comfort or safety. Bigger boats were often overcrowded. Police were tasked with inspecting to ensure the boats weren't overcrowded, but the boats would often take on additional passengers after inspection. Jean and Harold searched for life jackets to buy but didn't succeed. For one memorable outrigger trip to another island, rough seas forced them to go ashore and wait several hours in hopes of calmer waters. They finally got underway at nearly sunset. Jean marveled over the beauty of the sky, and then after night fell, they saw phosphorescent air bubbles each time the paddles dipped into the water. She could always find beauty in the things around her.

On this trip which was to stretch to nearly three months, the Carlbloms lugged a fair amount of baggage with them for their services. It was a long list: Jean's accordion, a public address system, a typewriter, a suitcase, tape recorder, radio, camera, and briefcase—as well as tracts and booklets to give out. They also included plastic covers to protect the accordion and P.A. system from the rain.

On each island, they were typically housed with a family, but there were often additional people who were helping in the services; and they hung around, even till midnight or later, talking and singing. They soon learned that Moluccan people are generally very musical, many playing the guitar and harmonizing. This was a contrast to the Central Java churches where Jean and Harold had ministered, which often had no musical instruments at all unless Jean had her accordion.

Some of these islands had no electricity, or if they did have electricity, it was unreliable, sometimes going off right as the service was starting, so kerosene lamps were kept at the ready.

Of course, there was never an indoor bathroom, and sometimes not even an outdoor one, other than the sea. Each morning they would walk down to the sea, where there were a couple of coves that would provide a little privacy, unless someone else was already there. In some places a little shelter—what we'd call an outhouse—was built out on a pier, with an opening to the water. To Jean it seemed to be such a place of beauty—a white sandy beach with clear turquoise water over coral beds—that it was a shame to see it used for human waste.

So many hardships accompanied this trip to remote areas, but Jean and Harold's daily journal entries showed that their focus was not on the difficulties, but on the results for God's kingdom. Jean always reported on the number of responses for salvation and for healing, and their daily times of prayer always focused on bringing souls into the Kingdom of God.

This was a very busy trip for them. Harold preached 96 times in 83 days! They held services nightly, as well as Sunday mornings. Some training times were also included. They were there to encourage some very small churches established years before by the pioneering Ralph Devin family.

Partway through the trip, near the tail end of 1971, Harold and Jean were delighted by the news of the birth of a fourth granddaughter. Charlaine and her husband Jerry were the proud parents of Jordana.

The Carlbloms returned from the lengthy trip in February to Djokja, with the challenge to find a new home in Salatiga. They traveled the 70 miles between the two cities too many times to count, searching for a house to live in and a building for a church. After one of these trips, they arrived home to a waiting telegram from her sister reading, "Our wee mother went to heaven." If one were to read the abundant love Jean expressed in so many letters home to her mother, it would be difficult to imagine how heartbreaking it must have been for her to be so far from her family at this time. Grandmother Ramsay had stood only four feet, eight inches high, but she was a giant in spiritual stature and had touched so many lives. Her faithful prayers, encouragement, and even admonitions would be missed.

Grief would have to be set aside. It was time to move. They soon moved to Salatiga and launched a campaign in nearby Ambarawa. The hall seating 400 was filled by the second week. More than 550 people accepted Christ during that campaign. In July their schedule included the Missionaries' Conference, Ministers' Seminar, and the National Church Congress. Then they rushed back to Central Java to begin the Bojolali (also Boyolali) campaign, which was in a temporary structure in front of a house that would be used for the church.

As if the month didn't already hold enough, two break-ins surprised them in July, when someone came in through the roof and the ceiling at their home. A number of needed items were stolen such as their typewriter, tape recorder, and some PA equipment; but the thing they felt worst about was an audiotape they had just received from home. It held the voices of their loved ones. The grandchildren had talked to them on the tape, along with their daughters and sons-in-law, and their daughters had sung on it. They listened to it over and over the day they received it, and it was stolen the very next day.

There was no time to lament the loss. They went to the Far East Conference in Hong Kong in August, attended by 160 missionaries and national church leaders. Rev. Phil Hogan and Rev. Thomas Zimmerman spoke. Although this meant taking time from their busy schedule of campaigns and establishing new churches, it was a much-needed time of spiritual refreshment. However, Jean spent four days in the hospital in Hong Kong. She had been sick before they left Salatiga, and the sickness returned with vigor during their trip. She was diagnosed with a severe, acute attack of bronchitis, along with gastritis, an infection of the intestines.

Thankfully she recovered enough to make the return trip on time. Immediately upon returning to Java, they began the campaign in Salatiga. Fully 430 people responded to the salvation call. Jean and Harold spent all day every Tuesday and Friday visiting homes, with a service at night in Salatiga. Wednesday they did visitation in Ambarawa with a service there that night, and Thursdays the same in Bojolali. On Sundays they rotated among the three churches. Even though they had a heavy schedule, Harold never neglected his prayer and study time.

However, the schedule was hard on them physically. At the end of October, poor Jean was still coughing, and Harold also had intestinal problems. Besides the services and visitation, Jean typically wrote 50 to 70 letters a month. Her letters were typewritten with very narrow margins. She didn't even like to use paragraphs, because it "wasted so much space." After the typing was finished, she typically wrote long-hand around any margin that remained, all along the side and at the top. Quite often she'd even use an Indonesian word here or there when she couldn't find an English word that expressed what she wanted. This worked fine for her daughters, who knew Indonesian, but sometimes her sister and others would be left to guess the meaning of a word. By then Harold was the Field Chairman, so he had his hands full with letters also, writing about the business of the whole field of Indonesia, as well as arranging for evangelists visiting the country.

The year of 1972 saw two more churches being planted, in Ambarawa and Bojolali. They continued the difficult schedule, glad to see the progress of each church. They always kept returning to the churches already established, in order to encourage the leadership and watch for trouble. An Indonesian presbyter was of great help to Harold, especially in the process of planting a church, as he knew which of the many permits would be needed as well as all the rentals they'd have to get.

Also, 1972 brought with it some changes. The Indonesian government instituted a reform in their spelling. All words and names that had previously included the two letters *dj*, such as *Djakarta* and *Djokjakarta* were to have the *d* dropped, instead making those words *Jakarta* and *Jogjakarta*. *Bandjarmasin* was changed to *Banjarmasin*. Spelling of place names had always been difficult, as—in a number of cases—several different spellings were acceptable. For example, *Menado* was accepted just as well as *Manado*.

The change in spelling was a minor matter. Back home, another change was happening, and a more important one: the number of Jean and Harold's grandchildren. After having four grandsons born in a row, and then four granddaughters, 1973 brought another grandson in Fond du Lac: Christopher Balken. The number would never matter. It could be eight or nine or a dozen; Jean and Harold's hearts always expanded with love for all of them.

While love could expand, they began to realize that energy didn't. In fact, the missions board in Springfield let them return to the U.S. in mid-October for a six-month leave because of the strenuous pace they'd been keeping. They did a couple of months of itineration and celebrated Christmas with the family in Fond du Lac. Jean had bladder surgery in February 1974, and by the end of April they were headed back to the field.

Chapter 11

Much Work, Illness, and Visitors: Seventh Term

Declare his glory among the nations, his marvelous deeds among all peoples. —Psalm 96:3

Early on, the Carlbloms visited Semarang to find property for the church they'd be planting. From there they went to Northern Sulawesi, where they had ministered in their second term. Harold spoke for the District Council and the Bible school graduation, as well as handling numerous evangelistic meetings. He preached 36 times in 27 days—in 18 different churches. Obviously, the pace hadn't slackened. Jean's oldest brother Bob, also a preacher, was visiting them in Indonesia at this time, and he preached in neighboring churches most of those same nights. Harold joked that they had doubleheaders those nights!

Harold was voted in as chairman of the Field Fellowship Committee again on the nominating ballot at the annual conference. The field committee consisted of five missionaries and a national executive team of five Indonesians. These committees met together, and advice was offered by the missionaries; but the nationals had been making the final decisions for some time then, as the goal was for the Assemblies of God in Indonesia to be led by indigenous peoples.

During the latter part of 1974, they ran seven successive weeks of services in different areas of Java. Whenever possible, they'd stay overnight with other missionaries who lived closer to where the services were taking place to avoid the stress of traveling by car. For a change it was nice not be worried about being forced off the road by an oncoming vehicle passing into their lane. They could be free of bicyclists, oxcarts, and people darting out into their path at any time. Besides, for some of these services, it was a two-hour trip each way.

The church in Semarang was planted around this time. A large sum of money had been donated by a family of Chinese doctors who were living in Michigan for a church building to be erected. The plan was to hold a campaign in a large hall first. The missionaries had found out through previous campaigns that Indonesian people were much more likely to attend services in a hall than in a church, so they generally met for several weeks in a hall, and then moved to have services in the church.

Due to political unrest at the time, the police canceled their use of the hall, so they had to begin services in the church, so it was a slow start; but they persevered. The Indonesian leadership asked Harold to pastor there until a suitable pastor could be found. When arrangements were made for the new pastor, the Carlbloms once again began evangelizing in other areas. The year ended with many accomplishments to count, but 1975 was to have a rough start.

Harold was struck by dengue fever in January and was left very weak. Always the willing worker, he attempted to get back to his schedule too soon—and relapsed. He was still quite drained after seven weeks, and it was more than ten weeks before he was able to get back to visitation and preaching—and even then he had to work up to it gradually. It made for a difficult year compared to previous ones, but they kept their eyes on

Jean and Harold's fortieth anniversary.

the Lord. As he recovered, April arrived, marking their fortieth anniversary, which they celebrated with other missionaries.

Jean and Harold were delighted to welcome her sister Barbara for a visit in November of 1975. They'd been urging her to visit them for years, and she finally was able to do it, together with Evie Spencer, a close friend. The Carlbloms were eager to show the pair at least a bit of the country.

Indonesia is a beautiful country with much greenery and many mountains (not tall enough for snow, but still lovely). Many of these mountains are volcanoes, as Indonesia is part of the Ring of Fire.

Although it's mountainous—and even with active volcanoes, the Indonesian people make use of all their land; so even in mountainous areas you can see beautiful rice terraces, making the most of the farmers' acreage. The vegetation is lush and green, and flowers are abundant. Bougainvillea trees and bushes provide bright splashes of color across the landscape. The air is fragrant with frangipani, jasmine, and agave.

They welcomed the opportunity to show more visitors their lush and lovely surroundings in January of 1976. Daughter Marjorie and her husband Bob arrived with Scott and Chère in tow. It was really a delight for Harold and Jean to be able to show their loved ones the country and the work they were doing there; and of course it was also a pleasure to introduce the Indonesian people to their family.

Other family news came from the U.S. Charlaine and her husband Jerry had divorced earlier; and she married Peter Stroukoff in February. At first they lived in Tennessee with Charlaine's daughter, Jordana; but eventually moved to Fond du Lac, Wisconsin, near other family.

There was also exciting news from Jean's sister Barbara. After 60 years of singleness, she took the big step and married a widower, Fred Halquist. Fred was a gentle and kind man who loved Barb well, calling her his "Barbie." They were very happy together, celebrating every month with an anniversary celebration, because, at their ages, they thought they would never reach their twenty-fifth anniversary. To their surprise, they were married well over thirty years!

Activities filled the next few months: the dedication of the Bible school in Salatiga, another campaign with evangelists from the U.S., the East Java District Council, Central Java Council, another campaign, and the Missionary Field Fellowship Conference. In July they held a week of evangelistic meetings in the Madiun church, which they had planted in 1963. What a joy it was to see the fruit of their labors! August brought another campaign, a water baptism with twenty baptized, Spiritual Emphasis Week at the Bible school in Salatiga, a child evangelism effort, and the All-Java Youth Camp. In October, after an intense time of ministry, they went home to America for a six-month furlough.

Chapter 12

Moluccas and West Papua: Eighth Term

The Lord has made his salvation known and revealed his righteousness to the nations ... all the ends of the earth have seen the salvation of our God. —Psalm 98:2–3

Furlough did not mean all rest! They had a full schedule of itineration, but it was good being back in the States to be with family and away from the constant demands of the mission field. Six months passed quickly, and they left for Indonesia again at the end of April 1977, heading back to Semarang for more meetings in Central Java.

Once again, they went to the Moluccan Islands—Ambon and Ceram, traveling mainly by outrigger canoes—and their feet. They held a one-week campaign in Manokwari, West Papua, New Guinea, reaching crowds of over two thousand people. During this trip, they only had one free day in six weeks. Well into their sixties, the Carlbloms credited God with giving them strength to persevere. Their passion for reaching people buoyed them to continue sharing the message of salvation in obedience to God's call on their lives. Healings came in these services also—some they saw at the time, and some they heard of later.

Harold and Jean had a strenuous year in 1978, with eleven different areas of ministry. They visited the island of Timor, which had already seen quite a revival. The story is told about in C. I. Scofield's book *A Mighty Wind*. They found the people very receptive, and they rejoiced over the healing of two children who had been born deaf and mute.

In May and June the Carlbloms spent five weeks in Kalimantan, the Indonesian portion of the large island of Borneo. They even saw the house where they'd lived when they first moved to Banjarmasin thirty years before. In letters home to her family, Jean reminisced about many things that had happened in that first home away from home. During this trip, they also stayed in some very primitive conditions—the most primitive yet. Jean wrote about it in a letter.

> *All the houses in those "kampungs" [villages] have only one room, and everyone slept on the floor on (woven) mats that we didn't know how many others had slept on before. We did bring a sheet and used it over us when it cooled down at night. Some places made a "toilet" for us, but that means they just cut a path into the woods to a secluded place (maybe at a distance of two or three blocks), dug a hole in the ground, and covered it with boards. It was generally quite muddy because of being freshly dug, and it was still raining in that area. Kind of hard to squat with arthritis besides being this age, so we had a time of it, but there was privacy anyhow, except for the pigs. We always had to carry a stick to ward them off. The houses are all made with rough, crude timber or of bark, with thatched roofs, but none are very tight. They have all the floorboards not quite meeting the walls so they can spit down to the ground beneath. They are built a meter above ground on stilts. You should see these people wiggle out of one set of clothes into another over at one side of the room—very modest. We couldn't quite do that but took ours to the bathing place to change, and that is something, too. It may be a stream, river, or spring out in the woods. You feel very much like Adam and Eve.*

In her diary she wrote about a little boy in the household who called them Adam and Eve. She wrote,

Moluccas and West Papua: Eighth Term

"We wondered if he saw us bathing!" They ate what the people ate, usually rice and sardines or fried rice, sometimes with boiled or fried sweet potatoes, often three times a day. Surprisingly, in some of these areas—even in what looked like a fertile place with a long growing season—they didn't have vegetables or fruit very often.

Also, no electricity was available in most of these areas, so they used kerosene lanterns. They washed their laundry at the springs when they went to take a bath—and then hoped the clothing would dry out quickly in the humid conditions. The simple one-room houses where they stayed on this trip contained a minimum of comforts, as Jean described in a letter:

> *We were served dinner while sitting on the floor feeling very stiff. Oh, for the limberness of some of these older Indonesians! They squat for hours it seems, with their feet flat on the floor and balance beautifully, or else they sit hugging their knees. I stretched my feet out straight, and my back hurts and knees get stiff. Then I sit sideways with my legs to the side, and I cramp up in no time. We sat on the floor there waiting for the people to gather for service.*
>
> *They had no chairs or stools to sit on for me to play the accordion. Finally they went to a neighbor's and came back with a low stool.*

Jean later wrote, "I was never in my life so glad to see a chair as after these meetings! There are no chairs in these houses!"

Sitting on the floor was only one of the physical hardships of this trip. Jean recounted a trip to one of their meetings:

> *We left on a Sunday afternoon, seven kilometers walking and in the rain. I was taken partway on the back*

of a bicycle, but Harold walked all the way, of course choosing his steps so as not to slip in the mud, sometimes straddling the narrow path to avoid deeper puddles. Riding on the back of a bicycle was a new experience for me. Here I sat with my umbrella trying not to poke the back of the preacher, and trying not to get it caught in the branches of low trees or bushes, for the path was very narrow and thick with foliage. I thought of Absalom getting caught in the tree and his horse going off leaving him hanging by his hair, and I visualized me getting my umbrella caught and being swished off the bicycle!

There were monkeys in the forest all around, and back in one area they come so close to the houses. In fact, one day a monkey came to Rugiat's (the local pastor) and stole five eggs from the kitchen, tucking one under each arm—one in his mouth, and one in each hand—and running off with his prize. He hid them quickly in the long grass below a nearby tree. He climbed the tree with one, broke open one end, tipped it up and let it run into his mouth, then scampered down the tree for each one, doing the same thing, looking back at Rugiat, who dared not run and get the others in the grass lest the monkey would pounce on him.

We found lots of tuberculosis in these homes, and with one room and someone coughing all night, we could visualize those germs filling the air we breathed and on our dishes standing in the open, and just had to plead the protection of the Lord. One old man told us he had coughed blood before, but not at the present time. He took care of three small babies each day while the mothers went to the fields to work. He ate with his fingers, as they all do. He would put some in his mouth, then make another small ball to go in the mouths of the children. Same fingers!

The Carlbloms had taken mosquito netting along and tried to hang it up around the bed so that they could sleep free of mosquitoes. However, they found that some of the houses had tiny ants that got in the bed, attracted by perspiration, which was inevitable in these hot, humid conditions. Of course, the ants would bite. Finally, after a few nights of this, they sprayed insect repellent by the door and windows, which brought relief. But when they sat outside confines of the house, the ants came at them again. Sometimes they slept on mats on the wood floor, and sometimes they were given a three-quarter sized bed. Often they'd sleep head to toe to have more room.

One house they stayed in was roughly five-by-four meters, made of wood and bamboo slats, held together with ties on the various poles and slats rather than nails. The house was built roughly one meter off the ground, with pigs and chickens penned underneath, ready to pounce on tidbits that fell through cracks in the floor.

Jean described in a letter the difficulty in trying to sleep at night. "We could hear the sounds of the woods, pigs grunting and moving about under the house. Toward morning the chickens are restless, noisy, and running around, as well as the pigs snorting, and little piglets squealing."

Along with uncomfortable accommodations on this trip, they found the work difficult. Occasionally the response in the services wasn't very good. Often the Protestant churches were very much against them. The Protestant churches there were originally Dutch Reform churches, but through the years, they had become very liberal. They even tolerated polygamy, drinking and smoking, even for the pastors. Protestant leaders sometimes threatened the children with bad grades in school if they attended Jean and Harold's campaigns, probably because they were afraid of losing some of their people to the Assemblies churches.

Another challenge for the missionaries was the large number of *dukuns* (witch doctors) in these areas. People feared them, as they threatened those who identified as Christian. Jean and Harold invested a lot of time in prayer that the powers of Satan would be held back. They typically began their days in prayer with the local leaders, and Harold always spent time later in the day—often several times—praying earnestly for God to move.

Difficult or not, every campaign comes to an end. After returning to Central Java, Harold and Jean held a one-week campaign in Solo, then headed to Central Sulawesi. Their first stop was in Soroako, a nickel mining town. Their accommodations were much different from what they had come from in Kalimantan. It was a mining company house, with air conditioning, an American bathroom, plus a refrigerator, washer, and dryer. What luxury! This place was significantly different from the rain-forest villages. The people employed by the mining company were well paid—even with paid vacations.

Their luxurious surroundings were short lived. From Soroako they went to a couple other communities in Central Sulawesi, but they generally saw dirt floors and crowded conditions. Jean told of an unexpected visitor one night in service just at the time of the altar call. "A chicken that was being chased by the people next door got into the church. It came flying in the window, then fluttered all over the church, cackling all the time, up on the platform and under the benches, until they finally chased him out the door!"

Loose chickens were the least of the problems. Jean told the family of one trip from Central Sulawesi to Ujung Pandang in South Sulawesi. It was a 16-hour trip over switchback roads. "Luli (the driver) showed us where a family went over the edge of the road and landed on the road below, rolled over it, and down again; all were killed. Another place he showed a bus that had gone over and into the river. Later still we came to a huge boulder as large as a small house that had come tumbling down from above and was perched at the edge of the road."

They traveled in the Molucca islands, once again on outriggers or even prows (larger canoes) from one place to another, sometimes on a trip of four to five hours. They held services on little islands that had no electricity, stores, schools—not even a doctor. While on one of these islands, they traveled from one village to another by walking up to 10 miles on uneven paths, sometimes through long grass. After arriving, Jean once found 20 to 25 insect bites on each leg and arm from the grasses. The bites swelled and itched, so the local women made a poultice. In these primitive conditions, with no doctors, people relied on folk remedies, which sometimes worked—but often didn't. In this case, it did not work! She was still itching several days later.

Even with the difficulties and inconveniences, bright spots came often. The Moluccan islanders are known to be musical, and Jean wrote in her journal about the children who were gathering before service: "The children, over 50 of them, gathered about an hour before service and sang two-part harmony. It sounded so nice, and how easily they sang the second part. Sometimes we even heard a third part."

Being a child on the island wasn't easy. Some islands had a school going up to sixth grade, but others had no schools at all. If a family wanted their children to have more schooling than was available locally, they'd have to seek out a relative or someone else on another island who'd be willing to take them in.

Many of the residents in these places had *kebuns* (fields) that they farmed with various crops: yams, coconuts, rice, and more. However, they had to stand guard to protect their harvest from raiding monkeys. Harold and Jean would have said that it wasn't much different from their work to protect the progress they'd made over the years in sharing the gospel—new church plants and indigenous pastors needed a lot of prayer to protect them from Satan's influences.

Jean and Harold were not letting age slow them down on their endeavors—in fact, they were experiencing the most primitive and adventurous conditions of their many years in missionary service. However, in their letters and logs, they recorded many more mentions of exhaustion and sickness by the time they were in their late sixties.

August 1978 found them attending the historic Far East Conference in Full Gospel Central Church of Seoul, South Korea. This church, the largest church in the world, was pastored by Paul Yonggi Cho. The largest church was a fitting place for a big event: The Assemblies of God Asian Missionary Association was formed at the conference.

Chapter 13

Central Sulawesi: Ninth Term

When anxiety was great within me, your consolation brought me joy. —Psalm 94:19

The whole family together on vacation. Back row: Bob Pearson, Bob Liebelt, Byron Balken, Dick Balken, Brent Balken, Melonie Balken, Peter Stroukoff. Middle row: Patsy Pearson, Steve Pearson, Marj Liebelt, Harold Carlblom, Joanne Balken, Charlaine Stroukoff. Front row: Kristie Pearson, Scott Liebelt, Chère Liebelt, Jean Carlblom, Heidi Balken, Christopher Balken, Jordana Stroukoff.

The Carlbloms returned to the U.S. for a furlough in April of 1979. During this time, they were able to take a family vacation with their daughters, sons-in-law, and grandchildren in Wisconsin Dells. They rented several cabins on a lake, filling their days with area attractions as well as swimming and water-skiing. Harold was an avid water-skier and tried to get all his kids and grandkids up on skis. Most of them did so, with the exception of Patsy, who had no desire to try, insisting that she didn't want to swallow half the lake just to please everyone!

After their furlough of 1979, they headed back to Semarang in Central Java in April 1980 for several weeks of evangelistic campaigns before their annual missionary conference. Following that, they left for more campaigns in Central Sulawesi, ministering to and encouraging small congregations in remote areas. There was so much need.

Even after decades in missionary service, they had come to expect the unexpected: like eating python meat for the first time. One of the villagers had killed the 9-foot-long python while it was in the process of taking a chicken. The chicken lived; the python did not. Later they were told of an 18-foot-long python that had been seen in their area.

While no snakes made their way into the houses where they stayed, they did have a lot of trouble again with tiny, biting ants. The tiny insects even got into clothes that were hanging or lying folded in the room. They found one time that these ants were coming out of a hole in the thin mattress.

In her next letter, Jean exclaimed, "I have a new understanding of the saying, 'You've got ants in your pants!'"

While they were in a little village called Kolonodale, they were invited to make a call on the village chief for the end of Ramadan, a Muslim holiday called *Idul Fitri*. They visited the chief, who was dressed and seated ceremoniously, and were offered some little cookies. This kind of visit was fairly commonplace for them because Indonesia has a number of regencies ruled by kings; and as they traveled, often they were expected to call on the king of the regency. In addition, the expectation was that they register with local police to receive permits for holding services.

Thankfully, receiving permits meant that their work could continue. In one campaign, a *cicak* (small lizard) fell from the ceiling and landed on the back of Harold's shirt sleeve while he was preaching. Jean saw it—and kept watching. Evidently the *cicak* was alarmed by all Harold's animated movements and afraid to move; it clung tightly through the continual gestures. When Harold got to the altar call, the little creature ran up onto his neck before he finally noticed it and shook it off. One can only wonder how many of his audience members were watching that little drama play out instead of listening to his words!

Over the years, they got used to the idea of unfamiliar bugs and lizards, but one thing that was hard to take in stride was the consistently poor transportation because it affected their work greatly. In remote areas, transportation was quite undependable. Harold would be told that a boat was coming in at a certain time, and maybe it would—but maybe it would arrive a day later. Even flights weren't always on schedule.

Once they waited a whole day for the MAF (Missions Aviation Fellowship) plane to pick them up in Beteleme and take them to the next town, Taliwan; but it had not come. Jean suggested that Harold find a way to the town on the back of a motorcycle heading that way, as they had already missed the first night of the planned campaign. She said she'd follow when another vehicle came through heading that way. The idea made sense to Harold, and he set out on what would be quite an adventure.

His description of the trip on the back of that motorcycle was distressing. He had to hang on for all he was worth to keep from flying off. But the notoriously rough roads were only the beginning of his troubles. When they stopped at a 15- to 20-foot span to cross on only a coconut log—he'd have to get off and cross on foot. Harold later estimated crossing nearly 60 of those treacherous logs in the roughly five hours of travel. He noted the journey in his log. "I'll not forget the prayer of our dear pastor at Beteleme, as he prayed with much feeling for this missionary of considerable age who was willing to take this harrowing trip for the work of the Lord. Well, though it was a grueling trip, I'd do it many times over for the joy of seeing one soul saved, and we've had many! Praise the Lord!"

Don't forget that Jean had to follow him—somehow. She would have her own story to tell. She was told there was a jeep going to Taliwan, so she was thankful for the ride. A preacher and his wife and another lady also piled into the vehicle.

They took a different route—with no coconut logs—but the road was no smoother. Jean was bounced around so much that, to stay put in the jeep, she had to hang on tightly—so tightly in fact, that her arm ached for days afterward. When they approached bridges with boards lying loosely across the spans, they had to get out so the planks could be adjusted to the width of the jeep's tires.

At one point, they rolled to a stop. The truck ahead of them had stalled. There was no way around. It looked as if it would be a long wait.

The preacher and his wife began walking. About ten minutes later, Jean was told the wait would still be long, so she decided that she should try to catch up with the couple. What a challenge! The narrow, uneven path that passed for a road was totally mucky. In many places she couldn't find a solid place to step and slogged through the slippery mud. She later recounted the hike in the log book.

> *It was in the middle of the jungle and after 5 p.m. so it was looking kind of dark. I began to feel very alone . . . maybe I'd fall in a rut and break a leg, maybe there will be snakes . . . why did I come? "Lord, calm me—I put my trust in You." Then I heard "Ooh hoo!" from behind; and was I ever glad to see the only other lady passenger. I found out later she felt impelled to follow this white "ibu" [mother] and take care of her. I was so glad to have a companion—it didn't seem so dark now. Soon the truck that had stalled came along, and then the jeep.*

With such difficulties in traveling and many meetings on the calendar, The Carlbloms were becoming weary and exhausted with the schedule. Harold's voice was consistently giving him trouble with hoarseness, to the point that he sometimes asked Jean to preach instead. For Harold, there was never any halfway measure—he preached his heart out, whether there was a large group or a small one. Jean often noted in the journal, "Harold preached with real anointing tonight." Jean was Harold's biggest fan, and he was hers. Difficult or not, they continued on, firm in their faith and knowing that God kept watch over them.

When they went to campaigns on these islands, they usually stayed with the local pastors, sometimes in a separate bedroom with a curtain for a door, but always with lots of activity and noise. Sometimes there were early morning prayer meetings—as early as 4:30. They visited with the pastors to encourage them, and often other villagers stopped in to talk to them, often requesting prayer or counseling. Sometimes they accompanied the pastor visiting the people from his congregation.

They tried to get a nap in the afternoon—for Harold it had become necessary, and Jean sometimes took naps just to have the chance to withdraw from activities and the constant visiting. Even Indonesians often took naps during the hottest part of the day.

As usual, the toilet was usually some distance from the house, sometimes in the woods nearby, and always the squat-type toilet, which was becoming more and more difficult with their age and arthritis.

Harold and Jean were able to tell lots of bathroom stories over the years, and one of them was onboard a boat. They embarked in the evening for a trip from the town of Doom to Sorong, (both in Irian Jaya, or Western New Guinea). This vessel was meant to carry 65 people, but over 200 were aboard ship. To go to the bathroom—there were only two for all those people—they had to climb over people who were lying on mats in the passageway, all the while trying not to step on anyone. On the other hand, they were thankful to have their own cabin. It was very small, and only one bunk had a clean sheet on it; but they were able to lock it when they left to go elsewhere on the ship. However, it couldn't be locked from the inside, and the first night, a drunk fellow walked in on them.

Even so, Jean focused on the positive. She wrote that the early part of the next day was beautiful. The sunshine made the water sparkle, and they saw a whale playing, spouting water and diving down with the characteristic tail splash at the end, "Just like he was trained at Sea World!"

During the second night, there was a commotion, and people calling, *"Manusia ke laut!"* (Man overboard!) It took a while to get the ship stopped and turned around, but thankfully they found the man and brought him aboard. Jean watched what she could see of the rescue from their small porthole.

When they returned from this trip, they began hearing of riots in Central Java with Chinese businesses being attacked. The Chinese people were generally business owners; and as successful people, they were targeted by discontented people. Jean and Harold were greatly concerned about the Koo family, who had been faithful members of the church in Semarang. Their business had been attacked. The Koos found windows broken and some other damages, but thankfully, nothing was stolen from inside.

While they were in Semarang, they lived at their own home and enjoyed spending time with Warsilah and Yohana, who had both worked for them previously. Jean and Harold had taken a great interest in both girls, encouraging them in their Christian walk and even encouraging them to attend Bible school and go into the ministry. Connecting on a personal level felt like such an important part of their ministry.

Jean wrote in her journal of one lady in one of these Central Java churches. "She took my hand and held it and kissed it. Nineteen years ago when we opened this work she came and has been faithful ever since. Warsilah was only five years old but remembers and always came—Yohana too. Praise God for these faithful ones, but praise Him too for new ones to take the place of those who have gone on or moved."

They visited many of the churches they had planted those many years before in Central Java and were encouraged that the congregations were remaining strong and reaching new people. Some churches struggled, as one might expect, and the Carlbloms did all they could to encourage these pastors.

Chapter 14

Sumatra: Tenth Term

Teach us to number our days, that we may gain a heart of wisdom. —Psalm 90:12

They went back to the U.S. in December 1980 for a brief furlough—not quite four months—and were back in Semarang in April of 1981. They held two weeks of services in Java before leaving for two weeks in Kalimantan, Borneo. What a blessing it was for them to meet one of the kids who had come to their first Sunday school in Banjarmasin in 1947; he was still serving the Lord.

Jean and Harold in typical Indonesian surroundings.

He'd been the only one of his family to follow Christ but was still faithful 34 years later. The Carlbloms did not always see the fruits of their labor, but God allowed it sometimes to encourage them. From Kalimantan, they went back to a month of services in East Java until the end of June, when they attended the Missionary Conference and National Congress.

During the National Congress of 1981, the nationals honored all the missionaries who had served in Indonesia for over 30 years. Margy Brown, along with Jean and Harold Carlblom, had served for 35 years. The Java district presented Jean and Harold with a map honoring them and showing the many churches they had opened in Central Java.

Harold spoke a few words to those gathered for the presentation. He drew Jean beside him, saying that she was always with him, being a blessing and a help. He told of the many miles they had walked together and the thousands of homes they'd visited, and of how tired he would get, but that Jean would urge him to go on for a few more. He expressed that they were not only inseparable in life, they were also inseparable in ministry.

Not long afterward, the Far East Conference was held in Singapore—a time of refreshing for them. It was a rare opportunity to be ministered to instead of pouring themselves out in ministry. Seemingly too soon, they headed back to Sumatra for six weeks.

In Sumatra, they saw many Batak houses typical of the region. A Batak house is long and built on stilts, and it has a roof that sweeps up on the end like the prow of a boat. One of the houses they visited wasn't a Batak house, but it was built up on stilts—and there was a buffalo kept under it! They always had to be ready for the unexpected.

Sumatra had several surprises in store. Typically in this area, the men sat on benches in church, but the women and children sat on mats on the floor. Because Jean played the accordion in the services, she was allowed to sit on a chair. Also, they needed a local interpreter sometimes while in Sumatra, for many of the people of this area spoke in the local dialect, and many did not even speak or understand Indonesian. Also, some of the women were fascinated by Jean, chucking her under the chin as you would with a child.

Though it was the rainy season in North Sumatra, they were scheduled for several nights of outdoor services in Kisaran. God kept the rain away, and they had around 2,000 people in the services.

When they were to leave one town for another and had to take a road that not even a jeep could navigate, Harold and the accompanying pastor and some other folks walked down the steep, rocky terrain, but they arranged for Jean to ride a horse, as they were concerned about her walking so far in the difficult conditions. They found a horse that had only been used to carry loads—not people—but Jean said, "I guess I'm a load!" She complied with their wishes, but even riding wasn't easy. She rode bareback as the horse's owner led the horse, but she had trouble slipping around on the horse's back, particularly going up or down a slope. Even so, they made it safely to the place where they were to catch the bus to go to the next town.

They got back to Java in October and spent their first day in 47 days with no meeting. After several strengthening days of rest, they continued on for two months of services in Central Java, excited to visit many of the churches they had established in the 1960s and connecting with the people they had come to care for so much.

Next came a schedule of 55 churches in eight months, some for full weeks, some for just a few nights. The constant interaction with people who wanted to visit with them became exhausting, especially with schedules that often began by 5:00 a.m. and continued till 10:30 or 11:00 p.m.

One big difference in Indonesia during this term was that they had no home base. Thus, on their infrequent breaks, they stayed with other missionary families such as the Lanphears, Woodses, Browns, and others—just to get a breather. Along with the Assembly of God missionaries, Harold and Jean also had strong friendships with other missionaries from the Christian Missionary Alliance and the Baptist church; and the Carlbloms always spoke highly of them. They visited back and forth with them and shared special times like birthdays and holidays. At these missionaries' rented homes, comfortable beds as well as American-style bathrooms were also much appreciated!

What a term it had been! Thankfully, Springfield approved a full year of furlough because of their heavy schedule. During this year (1982) in the States, Harold underwent carotid artery surgery, and shortly after that, the family noticed blood in his eye. They quickly took him to the doctor, who determined that he'd experienced a stroke—bleeding behind his eye. He needed another surgery. And because of the location of the bleed, Harold needed an expert in this particular surgery. Only two surgeons in the country were experienced enough for the job.

Harold left the next day for San Francisco, in the care of Jean and their son-in-law Bob Liebelt, to see one of these two doctors. After surgery, Harold had to be kept immobile for two weeks, so Jean and Bob explored San Francisco while they weren't with Harold.

Another significant event came that year. Charlaine's marriage to Peter had encountered problems, and they had divorced. She married Larry Henning from the Fond du Lac area in the fall of 1982, and they moved to the La Crosse, Wisconsin, area. Larry had a son, Matt, who enjoyed having another set of grandparents; likewise, Harold and Jean were thankful for the opportunity to get to know Matt and Larry.

November 1982 took Jean and Harold to Aurora, Colorado, where Harold was to be one of the speakers for the missions crusade at Aurora First Assembly, pastored by Howard Cummings. Rev. Cummings subsequently put together a book and a compact disc of messages from some of his favorite missionaries, entitled, *They Still Speak*, and Harold's sermon was included.

Chapter 15

Central Sulawesi and Irian Jaya: Eleventh Term

He will cover you with his feathers, and under his wings you will find refuge; his faithfulness will be your shield and rampart. —Psalm 91:4

The Carlbloms returned to Java by the sixteenth of December 1982, having celebrated an early Christmas with their family back in the States. They visited several services in churches they'd planted in Central Java years before, and Jean wrote, "We were thrilled to see so many—it brought tears of joy as we remembered scores and scores of visits trying to win some who never seemed to respond but are faithful now." She also mentioned how nice it was to see former Sunday school children helping to teach years later.

On a trip from Semarang to Salatiga, they took a bus whose driver was fast and careless. Jean wrote that he went like crazy, forcing other traffic off the road. She said, "I prayed a lot—so did Harold. But we are in God's hands—I did remind Him we have a work yet to do in Indonesia."

No long after returning from the States, they set off for services in Central Sulawesi on a variety of conveyances: first a small plane, then a crowded minibus, and finally on foot. At one point, to get to the next village, Korowou, they took a canoe downriver. Because of all their belongings, the canoe sat quite low in the water. Jean perched in the middle of the canoe; and when they went through rapids, some of the men got out to guide the canoe and keep it from overturning. But Jean, ever the optimist, wrote, "It was an interesting and delightful trip three and a half hours long."

The word optimistic was a good one to describe Jean, but soon her letters mentioned weak spells that Harold occasionally experienced. She was worrying that it could be heart problems or another stroke but trusting that God would keep them in His hands.

She told of one couple who asked Harold to dedicate their son to the Lord. When Jean and Harold had been there two and a half years before, they had attended this child's ritual shaving of his head, when the family was still Muslim. They had since turned from Islam and come to the Lord.

Jean had long made a practice of noting in her journal how many hands were raised for salvation and how many went forward for healing in every service. She also characterized the services and the responses as good, or not so good, but she trusted the results to the Lord. This Islamic family was one example of this—they had not responded at the earlier meetings, but a seed had been planted that eventually brought fruit.

Knowledge of that fruit and the hope for more made everyday inconveniences seem less important. For example, Jean described a *mandi* (shower room) that they used in Sulawesi: "What a bath house—curtained door flying open; an 8–10 inch opening between two boards on the side, which is not high; and another crack at the back, which has a view from the kitchen. I take a sarong with me and hang it over one crack, my towel over another, and my dress over another. I can't do anything about the cracks at the back and the other side—or the curtain door blowing open all the time."

It wasn't the only bathing issue during that term. In fact, Jean wrote about another bath experience in the next town.

> *We went to the river for our baths and took umbrellas in case it would rain. We walked half a kilo. We had to go down a small hill to the water's edge, and it was slimy with mud. We had such a time to get down to the water, and Harold slipped in. It became deep right away, and was soft and muddy, so we had difficulty even standing. I wore a sleeveless loose batik dress going in the water. It wasn't easy to keep our balance. The water was deep brown colored from the mud. So I wondered if we'd get clean at all. Before we finished it began to rain—our towels and clean underclothes were on a log above, getting wet. Harold pulled me up, both of us slipping and sliding in the mud. I decided to gather up my towel and semi-dry clothes and walk home in the wet batik. I held up two umbrellas over us while Harold dressed. He had bathed in his shorts and had to put on dry ones before he put on dry slacks. By then it was raining hard. P.T.L. anyway—we'll make it!*

And make it they did. They kept their focus on the Lord, and Harold preached from the heart. One of the towns they went to was Remboken, an area where they'd ministered many years before in Northern Sulawesi. Jean wrote of Harold's great freedom in speaking, and a precious anointing. "There was a wonderful response in prayer. The power of God in our midst was very strong. Many were filled with the Spirit or refilled, and many got a new touch from the Lord."

Tumaluntung was another town they visited, and they had an opportunity to spend an evening visiting with Mrs. Rooroh, the mother of Patsy's friend Loesje.

The church service there was full, and the response was good. Everyone attending this church was related in one way or another to the Rooroh family. Loesje was the first one to come to the Lord, back when she and Patsy were playmates and Patsy invited her to church. Her father then came to Christ, and gradually many of the family got saved. By the time of this visit in 1983, six or seven of them were already in the ministry.

During this term they also enjoyed a service in Tonsea Lama with the pastor, Hartimedes Pahu. He had been their first convert in Indonesia, and a favorite of the Carlblom girls while they were ministering in Banjarmasin, Kalimantan. After seeing him again, Jean wrote, "God does give us encouragement, letting us know some of the results of past meetings and some of the present. We do want to be used, and so long to see lives really transformed and filled with joy. And so many have told of finding Jesus in our meetings. God is so good. He does the work, and we are just instruments in His hands."

After all the services in Sulawesi, they flew in an MAF (Mission Aviation Fellowship) plane to Irian Jaya (Western New Guinea), going for the first time to the Central Highlands. In Wamena, the capital town of the Jayawijaya Regency, they saw people of the Stone Age Dani tribe—men wearing nothing but

Jean, Harold, and Hart.

waistbands and penis gourds and armbands above the elbow to ward away ghosts. One of them showed up in the doorway in one of their services, no doubt surprising Jean and Harold.

At the market, they noticed many of these tribesmen, who brought their garden produce to sell. The women generally wore grass skirts and little else. Jean had the opportunity to see the longhouses where the Dani people lived. There was a long house for cooking and eating. Then there were separate longhouses for men and for women, built with two levels—the level above for living, and the level below with fireplaces for warmth. The Carlbloms were not able to minister to the Dani people, because of the brevity of time there. Indonesia is the fourth largest country in the world by population, and there are hundreds of native ethnic and linguistic groups. The island of Java is home to more than half of the country's population, and that is why so much of the Carlbloms' time was spent in Java.

After Sulawesi, the next stop was visiting the Moluccas once again, then finishing March of 1983 with services in Surabaya before heading back to the States for furlough. On the way back, they were delighted for a stopover of several days in Rangoon, Burma, to visit Patsy's friend Loesje, who was stationed there at the Embassy with her husband, Dom. Always generous, she treated them to two days at a beautiful beach resort, and she accompanied them to do some sightseeing as well.

Furlough again brought rest, along with opportunities. Jean enjoyed volunteering at the Lighthouse Christian School in Fond du Lac. She had a natural gift for teaching the elementary students and had enjoyed helping all her daughters with correspondence school.

She seemed to be able to find just the right approach with children who had difficulty in different areas of learning. If one method wasn't working, she'd keep trying with other ways until the learning became easy.

But they weren't quite done with Indonesia—or maybe it was the other way around.

Chapter 16

Saying Goodbye

With your blood you purchased for God persons from every tribe and language and people and nation. —Revelation 5:9

A new year, 1984, took Jean and Harold to Sumatra for two months—mid-April through mid-June. Roads were notoriously bad there. While traveling on one bus, Jean counted 40 curves in ten minutes, then 45 the next ten minutes; and the following ten minutes brought 65 curves—many of them of the hairpin variety—with the driver going about 60 miles an hour! She did a lot of praying on that 30-minute ride!

While they had services in various areas of Sumatra, they'd hand wash (the only kind of washing available) their clothes and towels every day or every other day. On some islands, their local pastor or host would find someone to volunteer to wash for them, but in Sumatra they generally did their own. Then they'd have to hope the clothes would get dry before they had to pack again.

Not everything about this trip was troublesome. The bus ride to Sibolga was beautiful—Jean wrote about passing the rubber plantations and nut palm plantations, and seeing beautiful Lake Toba. She always appreciated the beauty of the countryside, and sometimes lamented that they couldn't stop and take a picture.

Their intent from the time they had planned this trip was to plant a church in the Sumatran city of Sibolga, so Harold had written the preachers in nearby towns, asking them to get the necessary permits and to rent a hall. However, when he arrived, he found that the preparations had not been made; and for several days they thought the planned services wouldn't happen at all—the hall they had planned on was not available anymore. Considering Harold's experiences in Indonesia, it seems that God must have always been working on improving Harold's patience. In Indonesia, as in many countries in other parts of the world, there's much less emphasis on schedules and timeliness. The expression is often used that they have *jam karet* (elastic time)!

Even after Harold was in Sibolga in person, they had many troubles getting all the necessary permits for services—it seemed the enemy was at work. Finally they got a permit for a different hall. However, three hours before service time, the hall had not yet been cleaned! In the end, they persevered. Jean wrote in her journal, "Well, praise the Lord—everything got arranged in time. The place was packed, and 75–100 people had to stand. And we had a tremendous altar call—maybe 70–75. P.T.L.!"

Following the services in Sumatra, they headed back to Java, and then to Tomohon in Minahasa for the congress, where Rev. Phil Hogan and Rev. Wesley Hurst from the States were both ministering. Jean reported that the services were so inspiring and uplifting, despite some tensions and difficulties during the business sessions and voting.

Following the congress in Minahasa in July, they headed back for more services in Central Java, just taking a few days off to visit Bali around their birthdays in August. Then they were back to business for services in Central Java again. Jean thanked God for the way He moved in the services, and also for the many testimonies of salvation and healings in past services.

The Carlbloms being led into the farewell service in Semarang.

As August shifted into September, Harold and Jean Carlblom began saying their goodbyes to leaders and congregations at the various churches for what they felt would be the last time; and it was an emotional point for them.

On September fifth, Jean wrote, "Today we leave our beloved Semarang." For almost forty years, they'd given themselves to ministry in Indonesia, investing in the lives of these dear people, and by this time Indonesia felt almost more like home than the States did. Only eternity will tell the results of their labor during these years.

If I Had Another Forty Years

Returning to the States, they settled into the home they'd bought in Fond du Lac and spent time with family. Jean was also able to go to the ladies Bible study and volunteer again at the Lighthouse Christian School. They were able to see Jean's sister Barb and her husband Fred, even traveling places with them. Another project of Jean's was to put together a loose-leaf book of Harold's poetry through the years; she looked through her photos to find an appropriate photo for each poem, as the poems often celebrated special moments.

In 1985, the Carlbloms celebrated their fiftieth anniversary in Minneapolis at the same church where they had first exchanged vows. Their daughters sang together, always a favorite with Jean and Harold. Jean's brother Charlie, who had been an artist and Christian cartoonist for over 50 years, shared one of his cartoon

Jean and Harold's fiftieth anniversary:
Charlaine, Marjorie, Harold, Jean, Patsy and Joanne.

Jean and Harold watching their daughters sing.

stories. Harold's sister Lorraine, who had been a recording artist, sang for the occasion. Other family members and many friends were there to congratulate them and wish them well. Their hearts were full as they rejoiced in God's blessings.

In late June of 1986, Jean and Harold were starting out on a big trip across the American West, hoping to connect with many of the friends they'd made through the years, as well as to do some sightseeing they had not been able to do during their busy furlough years. They'd always been on such a tight schedule that they had put sightseeing on hold. They stopped in Cold Spring, Minnesota, to spend a few days with Patsy and her family. While there, on Sunday morning, Jean approached Patsy, and told her that Harold wasn't feeling well and wouldn't be going to church, as he had "a kind of heavy feeling, and pain in his arm."

Patsy reacted quickly, telling Jean she'd take him to the Emergency Room immediately. It took a whole day for the hospital to determine that Harold was indeed having a heart attack. They recommended an angiogram to see where the blockage might be, but Harold wanted to go back to Wisconsin to have the test. If doctors needed to do bypass surgery, he wanted to be closer to home.

Harold recuperated a few days at the Pearson house, with their dog Scooter keeping him good company as he rested. Then they executed a plan to get Harold to Wisconsin, with Patsy driving Harold in the Pearson's car and Bob driving Harold's car, and then meeting Bob and Marj halfway to send Jean and Harold with them. After the necessary tests in Wisconsin, Harold underwent quintuple-bypass surgery in Milwaukee.

He recuperated well, his typical determination helping him. He still kept in touch with what was happening

Harold and Jean with Louise and Foster Woods.

in Indonesia, writing letters and praying for them and giving toward specific needs. When a man has given his energy, concern, and prayer for so long in one area, that concern continues.

They were able to take a modified trip out to the West Coast and were able to see missionaries Louise and Foster Woods, as well as other friends of long standing, many of whom had supported them through the years.

The following summer—1987—Patsy drove Jean and Harold to the annual family camp at Lake Geneva Bible Camp in Alexandria, Minnesota. In a Sunday afternoon missions service, a camp leader interviewed Harold. The memory is indelible in Patsy's mind: her father's words, as his voice broke and tears filled his eyes to overflowing, "If I had another forty years, I would gladly give them to the people of Indonesia!"

Epilogue, by Patsy

Precious in the sight of the Lord is the death of his faithful servants. —Psalm 116:15

Indonesia seemed to be in their blood. Their hearts still pulled them back to Indonesia for one short trip in 1989, with Dick and Joanne accompanying them for three weeks of their four-month trip. My parents traveled to churches in Central Java, the Moluccas, and Irian Jaya.

Mom wrote us in a letter, "We have been so happy that we decided to come because it has been such a blessing to us and an inspiration to see how God is working here. There was one church in both Sorong and Manokwari, and now there are several, and the main church is much stronger."

She continued, "We thank the Lord that He lets us see some of the results of our labors. We had so many who came up to us in Manokwari who said to us that they had been saved in one of our campaigns here."

Later that year, my husband Bob and I arranged to take Mom and Dad to the General Council of the Assemblies of God, which was held that year in St. Louis, Missouri. It was great for them to once again enjoy that great gathering of believers, reconnecting with friends from the ministry.

Dad still kept up a correspondence with leaders in Indonesia, wanting to know how God's work was going forward. His heart never let go of that country and its people, whom he loved.

As time passed, Dad experienced more physical problems—a brain bleed after a minor accident and hard bump on his head. This resulted in surgery to relieve the brain bleed, and it became necessary for him to have physical therapy. Eventually he entered a nursing home. The home that the family found to be the best for him was the Fond du Lac Lutheran Home. Mom faithfully went to be with him every day of the week except for her Bible study day, and the two of them became a familiar sight around the nursing home.

In 1997, my husband and I had the opportunity to make a trip to Indonesia. We visited Tomohon in Sulawesi, meeting one after another who told me that they had accepted Christ as their Savior or received the baptism of the Holy Spirit under my parents' ministry. They had a great respect for the spiritual legacy he had left there.

Then when Bob and I were visiting in Central Java, I was asked to speak at the Magelang church that my parents had started. What a blessing it was to see the long-lasting results of Mom and Dad's work there!

Dad's health continued to deteriorate, and in February of 1998, his body began to shut down. I went quickly from Minnesota to be with the family; and on that last evening of his life, we sang choruses and hymns, read Scripture to him, and told him we loved him, although he was not responding anymore. During the night Dad went to be with the Lord, and I'm sure he heard, "Well done, thou good and faithful servant!"

So many people gathered for his celebration service. One highlight of the service was when Dad's grandson Brent Balken and his wife Melonie sang a song written by Janet Paschal, "Another Soldier's Coming Home," which summed up Harold's life perfectly.

His back is bent and weary
His voice is tired and low
His sword is worn from battle
And his steps have gotten slow
But he used to walk on water
Or it seemed that way to me
I know he moved some mountains
And never left his knees

Strike up the band
Assemble the choir
Another soldier's coming home
Another warrior hears the call he's waited for so long
He'll battle no more
But he's won his wars
Make sure Heaven's table has room for at least one more
Sing a welcome song
Another soldier's coming home

He faced the winds of sorrow
But his heart knew no retreat
He walked in narrow places
Knowing Christ knew no defeat
But now his steps turn homeward
So much closer to the prize
He's sounding kind of homesick
And there's a longing in his eyes

(used by permission)

Mom missed Dad so much, and her health was beginning to fail, as well. She had macular degeneration, and Alzheimer's disease was taking hold of her thinking. We found someone to live with her, so she could remain in her home as long as possible. Eventually that became unfeasible, and she entered the same nursing home where Dad had been.

She'd often play the piano by ear for her fellow residents and remained her same cheerful self, even though her mind and memory were failing her. I remember going to see her. Her face would light up, and that wonderful smile would spread across her face; and although she couldn't remember my name or my relationship to her, she knew I was someone who loved her—someone whom she loved. She joined Dad at that heavenly table on March 10, 2008.

Two lives, dedicated to God and His work and given without reservation, will always leave a legacy of faith in the lives of their family and all who knew them. Though they were imperfect, as we all are, they served the Lord who loved them and called them to do as best they could. Eternity alone will show the effect of their lives.

Acknowledgements

I want to say a special "thank you" to Renee Garrick for your careful editing, fact-checking, and suggestions—you were always sensitive to how I wanted to describe something. I do appreciate your expert help throughout the process. I know that it's a better book because of you!

Thank you also to Carol Lenning and Pat Webster for your encouragement along the way—you made me feel like I could be a real "author."

Thanks to my sisters Marj Liebelt and Charlaine Ramsay for jogging my memories and contributing your own, and thanks to Loesje Lanphear and Bud Brown for answering my questions about various events and places.

I also owe a debt of gratitude to my mom for keeping such meticulous records in her logbooks, as well as the wealth of information from her letters. Without them, there would be no book!

Glossary of Indonesian Words

adat: custom or tradition
abu: volcanic ash
atap: palm leaves sewn together for a thatched roof
bak: cement tank
batak: house with roof curved up at each gable end
beca: bicycle-driven mini taxi
bendi: horse-drawn taxi
Dayak: a local tribe of Borneo
djongas: hired man
dukun: witch doctor
gado-gado: salad
hukum tua: village elder
ibu: mother
jahat: wicked
jam karet: elastic time
kamar kecil: toilet room
kampung: village / neighborhood
kebun: field
lemari: wardrobe / cabinet
mandi: shower room
manusia ke laut!: man overboard!
Mesdjid: mosque / Muslim prayer house
orang hutan: person of the forest
rupiah: Indonesian money
sate: skewered, grilled meat
tjelaka: accident / mishap
tjitjak (now cicak): small lizard / tropical house gecko
tuan: mister

Indonesian Place Names

Ambarawa (town in Central Java)
Ambon (Moluccan island)
Bali (island of Indonesia)
Bandjarmasin, now spelled Banjarmasin, nicknamed Bandjar (city in Borneo)
Bandung (city in West Java)
Barito (river in Borneo)
Beteleme (town in Central Sulawesi)
Bojolali, also Boyolali (town in Central Java)
Borneo, now named Kalimantan (island of Indonesia)
Celebes, now called Sulawesi (island of Indonesia)
Ceram (Moluccan island)
Djakarta (capital city of Indonesia, in Java)
Djokjakarta, called Djokja for short (city in Central Java)
Doom (town in Irian Jaya)
Irian Jaya (Western New Guinea)
Java (most populous island of Indonesia)
Kahaian, now Kahayan (river in Borneo)
Kalimantan, previously called Borneo (island of Indonesia)
Kapuas (river in Borneo)
Kisaran (town in North Sumatra)
Klaten (city in Central Java)
Kolonodale (town in Central Sulawesi)
Korowou (town in Central Sulawesi)
Kuala Kapuas (town in Kalimantan)
Langoan, Minahasa (town in Sulawesi)
Madiun (city in Central Java)
Magelang (city in Central Java)
Makassar, now Ujung Pandang (city in Sulawesi)

Malang (city in East Java)
Manado, also Menado (city in Northern Sulawesi)
Manokwari (town in Irian Jaya)
Martapura (river in Borneo)
Minahasa (region in Northern Sulawesi)
Moluccan Islands, Moluccas (Now Maluku Islands,
 a.k.a. Spice Islands)
Muntilan (town in Central Java)
Pulang Pisau (village in Borneo)
Remboken (town in Northern Sulawesi)
Salatiga (city in Central Java)
Selecta (resort above Surabaya, Java)
Semarang (city in Central Java)
Sibolga (town in Sumatra)
Solo (city in Central Java)
Soroako (nickel mining town in Central Sulawesi)
Sorong (town in Irian Jaya)
Sulawesi (island of Indonesia)
Sumatra (island of Indonesia)
Surabaya (city in East Java)
Tjimahi (city in West Java)
Tomohon (town in Northern Sulawesi)
Tonsea Lama (town in Northern Sulawesi)
Tumaluntung (town in Northern Sulawesi)
Ujung Pandang (city in South Sulawesi)
Wamena (capital of Jayawijaya Regency in Irian Jaya)

Made in the USA
Monee, IL
15 November 2020